THE PROMPT
RECIPE

THE PROMPT RECIPE:

A Practical Guide to Prompt Engineering and AI Interaction

AHMED BOUCHENTOUF

Table of Contents

Introduction

Artificial intelligence is everywhere. Suddenly, it feels less like science fiction and more like... Tuesday. Tools like ChatGPT haven't just arrived; they've exploded onto the scene, breaking user adoption records faster than any technology in history. A revolution is undeniably underway, promising to reshape how we work, create, and even think.

You see the potential. As a high-achieving professional – a consultant, a director, an entrepreneur, an expert in your field – your mind naturally gravitates towards leverage. You envision AI streamlining your analyses, drafting communications, brainstorming strategies, freeing up precious hours, and perhaps even unlocking new levels of creativity and insight. The promise is intoxicating: doing more, better, faster.

And yet... there's a nagging dissonance. A gap between the hype and your daily reality.

You've tried it. You've experimented with prompts, asked questions, delegated tasks to your new digital assistant. Sometimes, the results are intriguing, maybe even helpful. But often? They're underwhelming. Generic. Vague. Occasionally, outright wrong. You ask for a market analysis, and you get a Wikipedia summary. You request creative ad copy, and it spits out clichés. You hope for a strategic insight, and it offers platitudes.

The experience leaves you with a familiar feeling, one echoed by countless peers: frustration.

Think of the strategy consultant in Paris, drowning in data, dreaming of automating 30% of their analysis workload, only to find the AI's output requires more time to fix than it saves. Or the marketing director in Tokyo, who sees the *potential* for quality content generation but feels stuck, admitting, "without the right prompts, it's just noise". Consider the e-commerce entrepreneur in New York, hoping to internalize content creation for product descriptions and emails, but finding the AI's first drafts consistently miss the mark, lacking the brand's voice or persuasive edge.

They, like you, recognize the immense power simmering beneath the surface of these tools. They see colleagues, perhaps, or read articles showcasing impressive feats of AI-driven productivity and creativity. But translating that potential into consistent, high-quality results in their own workflow remains elusive. It feels like being handed the keys to a supercar but finding yourself stuck in first gear, engine sputtering, unsure how to unleash its true power.

This gap, this friction between the promise of AI and the often-mediocre reality of its output, breeds a quiet skepticism. Is it overhyped? Is it really ready for prime time in demanding professional contexts? Is the problem... the tool itself?

Here's the crucial realization, the first step towards bridging that gap: **The problem usually isn't the tool. It's how we're using it.** More specifically, it's how we're *asking*.

Let's try a quick self-diagnosis. On a scale of 1 to 5, where 1 is "Very Dissatisfied" and 5 is "Very Satisfied," how would you rate your current satisfaction with the results you typically get from generative AI tools like ChatGPT?

Take a moment. What number comes to mind?

Now, more importantly, *why* did you choose that number? What are the main reasons for your current level of satisfaction or dissatisfaction? Are the outputs too generic? Not specific enough? Lacking insight? Full of errors? Do they fail to capture the right tone or style? Do they require significant editing?

If you rated yourself less than a 4 or 5, know this: you are far from alone. Your experience mirrors that of countless driven, intelligent professionals wrestling with the same paradox. They see the potential, they feel the frustration, and they sense there *must* be a better way.

The good news? There absolutely is. The solution isn't about waiting for the next AI model or finding some secret setting. The power to unlock consistently superior results, to truly harness this revolution for your specific needs, is already within your grasp. It lies in understanding and mastering the art of the prompt.

But what exactly *is* a "good" prompt? Where does the disconnect between the promise of AI and the reality of its output truly originate? Often, it stems from a fundamental misunderstanding of how to communicate effectively with this new form of intelligence, fueled by a pervasive and misleading myth.

The Alluring, Empty Promise of the "Magic Prompt"

In the early days of any powerful new technology, there's a natural tendency to look for shortcuts, for silver bullets.

With generative AI, this manifests as the quest for the "magic prompt".

We see it everywhere – articles promising "10 ChatGPT prompts guaranteed to make you rich," LinkedIn posts sharing "secret formulas" to unlock AI superpowers, online courses hawking templates purported to solve any problem. The allure is undeniable: just copy and paste this perfectly crafted incantation, this secret sequence of words, and *poof* – the AI will deliver exactly what you need, effortlessly.

We hunt for these magic words, hoping to stumble upon the "Open Sesame" that unlocks the treasure trove of AI capabilities. We bookmark promising examples, subscribe to newsletters filled with prompt libraries, and experiment with borrowed phrases, hoping one will finally crack the code.

But what if this entire quest is fundamentally flawed? What if chasing the magic prompt is not just inefficient, but a complete dead end?

Consider this: the very idea of a single, universally perfect prompt ignores the fundamental nature of both our needs and the AI itself. Your specific goals, context, and desired outcomes are unique. The prompt that works wonders for generating marketing slogans for a tech startup is unlikely to be ideal for drafting a nuanced legal clause for a notary or summarizing complex project updates for an IT manager. Needs vary wildly.

Furthermore, the context is constantly shifting. New information emerges, project requirements evolve, target audiences change. A "perfect" prompt from last week might be obsolete today. And the AI models themselves are continually updated, subtly changing how they interpret and respond to certain instructions. A static formula simply can't keep pace with this dynamic reality.

More fundamentally, however, the myth of the magic prompt misunderstands what AI actually *is* and *does*. These large language models (LLMs) are not sentient beings understanding your intent in a human way. They are incredibly sophisticated pattern-matching machines. They work by predicting the most statistically probable next word (or token) based on the sequence of words they've already seen – including your prompt.

Think of it like the world's most advanced auto-complete. When you type "The cat sat on the...", your phone suggests "mat," "roof," or "sofa" based on common patterns in language. AI does something similar, but on a vastly larger scale, drawing on the trillions of words it ingested during training.

This leads to a critical, unavoidable principle, an adage as old as computing itself: **Garbage In, Garbage Out (GIGO)**.

If your input – your prompt – is vague, ambiguous, poorly structured, or lacks crucial context (garbage in), the AI's output will inevitably reflect that. It will likely be generic, irrelevant, confusing, or simply unhelpful (garbage out). The quality of the output is inextricably linked to, and fundamentally limited by, the quality of the input. The AI doesn't magically intuit your needs; it mathematically processes your instructions.

As one expert aptly put it, "ChatGPT is a reflection of the prompts we provide". It mirrors your clarity or your confusion. It executes your instructions, flawed or flawless, with remarkable fidelity.

This literalness is often best understood through an analogy: **Imagine the AI as a powerful, slightly mischievous Genie in a lamp**. It can grant almost any wish (fulfill almost any request), but it interprets your words with absolute literalness. Ask for "a million bucks," and you might get a million deer (male bucks) delivered to your doorstep, or perhaps a million dollars in Monopoly money. Why? Because your wish was ambiguous. You didn't specify *currency* or *real* money. The Genie executed the request faithfully, but the imprecision of the wish led to a useless, perhaps even disastrous, outcome.

It's the same with AI prompts. A poorly formulated request – one that's vague, assumes context the AI doesn't have, or uses ambiguous language – will lead the AI down a statistically plausible but ultimately incorrect or unhelpful path. It's not being difficult; it's simply operating according to its nature, reflecting the imprecision of the instructions it received.

The quest for the "magic prompt," therefore, is a search for something that doesn't exist. There is no secret phrase that bypasses the need for clear thinking and precise instruction. There is no shortcut to quality.

But this isn't bad news. In fact, it's incredibly empowering. Because if the quality of the output depends directly on the quality of the input, it means the control lies firmly in *your* hands. You are not passively subject to the whims of an opaque algorithm. You are the director, the architect, the one holding the wishing lamp. The power to elicit brilliance from the AI rests squarely on your ability to formulate your requests effectively.

So, if the answer isn't a magic formula to be found, but a skill to be developed, what exactly *is* that skill? What truly separates a frustrating AI interaction from a remarkably productive and insightful one?

The Real Secret: Prompting Isn't a Formula, It's a Thinking Strategy

Here lies the core idea, the central insight that unlocks the true potential of generative AI, the keystone upon which this entire book is built:

"A good prompt is not a magic formula; it is a strategy of thought."

Let that sink in. The secret to consistently getting exceptional results from AI doesn't reside in finding the perfect combination of keywords or copying a clever template someone else designed. It's not about "hacking" the AI or discovering some hidden linguistic trick.

Instead, the power lies in the *thinking* that happens *before* you even type a single word into the prompt box. It's about the cognitive and strategic effort you invest in clarifying your intention, structuring your request, anticipating the AI's interpretation, and guiding it towards the desired outcome.

Mastering the art of the prompt, therefore, is fundamentally about mastering your own thinking process. It involves:

1. **Clarifying Your Intention:** Knowing *exactly* what you want to achieve. What specific information do you need? What task do you want the AI to perform? What should the final output look like, feel like, and accomplish? This requires moving beyond vague notions ("analyze this market") to precise objectives ("identify the top 3 competitors in market X based on criteria Y and Z, presented in a table format").

2. **Structuring Your Request:** Organizing your thoughts and instructions in a logical sequence that the AI can easily follow. This means providing necessary context upfront, clearly defining the task, specifying the desired format and tone, and outlining any constraints or crucial elements.

3. **Anticipating the Response:** Considering how the AI might interpret your instructions, identifying potential ambiguities, and preemptively addressing them. It involves thinking like the "Genie" – how could this request be misunderstood if taken literally?

4. **Guiding the AI:** Using precise language, providing relevant examples, and employing specific techniques (which we'll explore throughout this book) to steer the AI towards the high-quality output you envision.

This approach elevates prompting from a mere technical input task to a **strategic cognitive skill**. It's less about knowing *what* words to type and more about knowing *how* to think *before* you type. It's about applying the same intellectual rigor and strategic foresight to your AI interactions as you would to any other critical professional task.

Contrast this with the "copy-paste" or "prompt hacking" mentality. While borrowing ideas can be a starting point, relying solely on pre-made prompts without understanding the underlying thinking strategy is like trying to build a house using someone else's blueprints without knowing anything about architecture or engineering. It might stand up initially, but it lacks a solid foundation and won't be tailored to your specific needs or context.

The French philosopher Voltaire is famously credited with saying, "Judge a man by his questions rather than by his answers". In the age of AI, we might adapt this: **Judge the effectiveness of an AI interaction by the quality of the *prompt* rather than just the initial answer.** A well-crafted prompt, born from clear strategic thinking, sets the stage for a high-quality response, even if it takes a little iteration (more on that later). A lazy or vague prompt almost guarantees a mediocre outcome, no matter how powerful the AI.

Consider this: How do you typically approach a complex problem or a challenging task in your professional life? Do you dive in headfirst without a plan? Or do you pause, define the objective, break down the problem, consider different angles, and map out a strategy? Most likely, you apply a degree of structured thinking and planning.

The question then becomes: **Are you applying that same level of rigor and strategic thought when you interact with AI?** Or do you treat it more casually, firing off quick questions and hoping for the best, reverting to the search for that elusive "magic prompt"?

This book is designed to bridge that gap. It won't just give you a list of prompts to copy. It will teach you *how to think* so you can craft your *own* powerful prompts, tailored to your unique needs and goals. It's about shifting your paradigm – moving from hoping for magic to employing a deliberate, repeatable strategy. It's about transforming your interaction with AI from a frustrating game of chance into a predictable process for generating value.

To make this shift more tangible, let's embrace a central metaphor that will guide us throughout our journey...

From Hasty Cooking to Precision Pastry: Your Prompting Transformation

Think about crafting a prompt like cooking.

Anyone can throw a few ingredients into a pan, turn on the heat, and produce something edible. It might be a quick stir-fry, an improvised pasta dish – functional, perhaps even satisfying in a pinch. This is like crafting a basic, quick prompt. You toss a few keywords at the AI, ask a simple question, and you get... something. A response that's vaguely related to your topic, maybe usable with heavy editing, but rarely impressive. It's the "kitchen sink" approach – quick, messy, and yielding results that are just... okay. You've made a meal, but nobody's asking for the recipe.

Now, contrast that with the art of exceptional pastry. Think of a delicate macaron from Pierre Hermé, a multi-layered entremets from a master pâtissier, or even a perfectly laminated croissant. These creations aren't accidents. They are the result of **precision, method, understanding, and meticulous attention to detail**.

The pastry chef doesn't just "wing it." They:

- **Understand their ingredients:** The quality of the flour, the temperature of the butter, the specific type of chocolate – each element matters.
- **Follow a precise recipe (structure):** Steps are executed in a specific order, quantities are measured exactly.
- **Master their techniques (the 'tour de main'):** They know *how* to fold the batter, *how* long to whip the egg whites, *when* to chill the dough.
- **Control the environment (the oven):** They understand how heat and humidity affect the outcome and adjust accordingly.
- **Iterate and refine:** They taste, they adjust, they learn from subtle variations to perfect their craft.

The result isn't just "edible"; it's an experience. Elegant, refined, often seemingly magical, yet built entirely on a foundation of rigor and deep understanding.

This is the transformation this book aims to guide you through. We will move **from the rough-and-ready "kitchen cooking" of basic prompting to the "precision pastry" of strategic prompt engineering**.

This metaphor directly illustrates our insight: exceptional results require more than just throwing ingredients (words) together. They demand a *thinking strategy*. The pastry chef succeeds not because they found a "magic recipe" online, but because they understand the *principles* of chemistry, technique, and balance that make the recipe work. They think like a chef.

Let's visualize this. Picture a simple, home-baked yogurt cake made quickly on a Sunday afternoon. Pleasant, familiar, does the job. Now, picture that exquisite, jewel-like macaron, with its delicate shell, perfect "foot," and luscious filling. The difference isn't just taste; it's the entire *process* – the planning, the precision, the understanding, the skill involved.

That leap in quality, methodology, and strategic thinking is precisely the leap we will make together in the realm of prompting. We will dissect the process, understand the "ingredients" (context, keywords, instructions), learn the "recipes" (structured prompt templates), master the "techniques" (phrasing, iteration, providing examples), and understand our "oven" (how the AI model actually works).

This pastry metaphor will be our recurring guide, reminding us that crafting powerful prompts is an art grounded in science, a creative endeavor built on a foundation of rigor. It's about moving beyond hopeful guesswork to deliberate, skillful execution.

Are you ready to trade in your apron from the "kitchen sink school of prompting" for the toque of a strategic "prompt pâtissier"? Are you ready to learn the methods that transform frustrating interactions into consistently impressive results?

Excellent. Let's outline the journey we are about to embark on together.

Your Path to Prompt Mastery: What This Book Will Equip You With

This book is not just a collection of tips and tricks. It's designed as your **accelerated training program, your apprenticeship in the art and science of strategic prompt engineering**. It provides a reliable, repeatable method to transform how you interact with AI, moving you from inconsistent results to confident mastery.

Our journey is structured logically, following the progression from understanding the fundamentals to developing advanced techniques, all framed by our pastry metaphor:

1. **Understanding Your Ingredients and Your Oven (The AI Itself):** Before you can bake, you need to know your flour from your sugar and how your oven behaves. Here, we'll demystify the AI.

We'll explore *how* Large Language Models actually "think" (or rather, predict), why certain instructions work better than others, and why the "Garbage In, Garbage Out" principle is non-negotiable. You'll learn to see the AI not as a magic box, but as a powerful, logical system you can learn to influence effectively. *(Corresponds to Chapter 1)*

2. **Knowing What You Want to Bake (Clarifying Your Intention):** The best recipe in the world is useless if you don't know what dish you intend to create. This section focuses on the crucial, often-overlooked step of clarifying your *own* thinking *before* you prompt. We'll cover techniques like defining SMART(E) objectives and using the journalist's 5W+H questions to ensure you know exactly what you're asking the AI to do. You'll learn why "thinking" is the most critical ingredient in any successful prompt. *(Corresponds to Chapter 2)*

3. **Writing the Recipe Card (Structuring Your Prompt):** A great pastry recipe isn't a jumbled list; it's structured logically. Here, you'll learn how to structure your prompts for maximum clarity and impact. We'll introduce a simple yet robust template (like C.R.O.F.T.C. - Context, Role,

Objective, Format, Tone, Constraints) to ensure the AI receives all necessary information in the right order, minimizing the chance of it ignoring crucial instructions. *(Corresponds to Chapter 3)*

4. **Mastering the Details (Precision in Language and Format):** The difference between a good pastry and a great one often lies in the details – the exact grammage, the specific technique. Similarly, subtle choices in your prompt's wording, tone, style, and requested output format can dramatically alter the result. We'll delve into choosing precise verbs and adjectives, defining the 'how' (tone, style, perspective), specifying output formats (lists, tables, JSON), using constraints effectively, and even leveraging the power of examples ("few-shot prompting"). This is where you learn the "prompt pâtissier's" refined techniques. *(Corresponds to Chapter 4)*

5. **Tasting and Adjusting (The Art of Iteration):** No chef gets a complex recipe perfect on the first try. They taste, adjust, and refine. Prompting is the same. This section demolishes the myth of the "perfect first prompt" and embraces iteration as the norm. You'll learn how to analyze the AI's response

critically, diagnose shortcomings, and skillfully reformulate your prompts or use follow-up questions to guide the AI towards excellence in a collaborative dialogue. *(Corresponds to Chapter 5)*

6. **Creating Your Signature Recipes (Building a Prompt Library):** Great chefs develop their own signature dishes and reliable base recipes. Similarly, you'll learn how to identify your recurring needs and create reusable, adaptable "prompt patterns" or templates for common tasks like summarizing, brainstorming, or comparing options. We'll cover how to build, refine, and organize your personal library of effective prompts for maximum efficiency. *(Corresponds to Chapter 6)*

Throughout this journey, you don't need a background in computer science or linguistics. This book is designed for smart, busy professionals who want practical, actionable strategies they can implement immediately. The focus is on clear thinking, structured communication, and strategic application – skills you already possess and hone daily in your field.

Your Goal:

Before we dive in, take one more moment for reflection. Engage with this process actively. What is **ONE specific, meaningful goal** you want to achieve by mastering the art of the prompt?

Perhaps it's automating the first draft of your weekly reports to save 3 hours. Maybe it's consistently generating high-quality blog post ideas that resonate with your target audience. It could be using AI to analyze competitor strategies more effectively or to quickly synthesize complex research papers.

Write it down. Keep this goal in mind as you read. It will serve as your personal North Star, making the concepts and techniques more relevant and motivating.

You already possess the intelligence and strategic mindset required. This book will provide the missing piece: the **method**, the **understanding**, and the **tools** to bridge the gap between AI's potential and your desired results. By the end, you won't just be *using* AI; you'll be *dialoguing* with it effectively, strategically, and confidently – like a master pastry chef commanding their kitchen.

Let's begin our apprenticeship. Our first step? To truly understand the nature of our most important "ingredient" and our crucial "oven" – the AI itself. Let's peek behind the curtain...

1 - Inside the AI's Mind

Why Your Prompts Fail (and How to Fix It)

Before a master pastry chef even thinks about combining flour and butter, they understand their tools. They know the quirks of their oven – where the hot spots are, how quickly it heats, how dry or humid it runs. They understand their ingredients – how different types of sugar caramelize, why chilling dough matters, the precise role of yeast or baking soda. This deep, almost intuitive understanding isn't just trivia; it's fundamental. It's what allows them to move beyond simply following a recipe to truly *creating* – anticipating reactions, making subtle adjustments, and ultimately achieving results that seem effortless but are grounded in knowledge.

Interacting with Artificial Intelligence, especially powerful Large Language Models (LLMs) like ChatGPT, requires a similar foundational understanding. If we treat the AI like an inscrutable black box, blindly feeding it prompts and hoping for the best, we're essentially baking blindfolded. We might occasionally get lucky, but consistent, high-quality results will remain elusive. Our frustration, like that of the consultant drowning in data or the marketing director getting "noise" instead of signal, stems largely from interacting with a powerful system without grasping its basic operating principles.

This chapter pulls back the curtain. We're not going to delve into complex computer science or dizzying mathematics. Instead, we'll build a clear, practical mental model of *how* these AI systems "think" – or more accurately, how they process information and generate responses. Understanding this "oven" is the first crucial step towards crafting prompts that work *with* the AI's nature, not against it. You'll discover why some prompt formulations are dramatically more effective than others, grasp the inherent limitations you need to account for, and learn to adopt the most productive mindset for this new kind of dialogue.

Just as the chef understands *why* folding egg whites gently creates a lighter soufflé, you'll soon understand *why* structuring your prompt in a certain way leads to a more insightful AI response. Let's start with the most fundamental concept: what AI is actually doing when it answers your questions.

AI Doesn't "Understand," It "Predicts": The Supercharged Autocomplete

Imagine the autocorrect or predictive text feature on your smartphone. You start typing a sentence, perhaps "Let's meet for coffee at...", and your phone suggests "noon," "the usual place," or "3 PM." How does it do this? It has learned, from vast amounts of text messages, emails, and web pages, which words are statistically likely to follow the sequence you've just typed. It's not understanding your *desire* for coffee; it's simply calculating probabilities based on patterns in language.

Now, imagine that predictive text capability amplified billions of times, trained on a colossal dataset encompassing a significant portion of the internet, books, articles, and other texts – trillions of words in total. That, in essence, is what a Large Language Model like ChatGPT is doing.

When you provide a prompt, the AI doesn't "understand" the meaning in the way a human does. It doesn't grasp concepts, feel emotions, or possess beliefs. Instead, it performs an incredibly complex statistical feat: **it predicts the most likely next "word" (or, more accurately, "token" – often a part of a word) to follow the sequence of text it has seen so far (your prompt, plus**

any preceding conversation). It generates the first token, adds that to the sequence, then predicts the next most likely token, and so on, word by word, until it reaches a stopping point (like a length limit or a signal that the thought is complete).

It's a sophisticated pattern-matching and sequence-prediction engine. Its brilliance lies not in consciousness or comprehension, but in its staggering ability to internalize the patterns, structures, styles, and relationships within human language, gleaned from its immense training data. It knows that "peanut butter" is often followed by "and jelly," that legal documents tend to use certain phrases, and that Python code follows specific syntax rules – all based on statistical probability.

Think about it: type the beginning of a famous phrase like "To be or not to be..." into a search engine. What does it suggest? Almost certainly, "...that is the question." The search engine isn't pondering Hamlet's existential dilemma; it's recognizing a common sequence and predicting the statistically most likely completion. LLMs operate on a similar principle, just with exponentially more data and computational power, allowing them to generate coherent, contextually relevant, and often remarkably human-sounding text.

This fundamental mechanism – prediction, not comprehension – has profound implications for how we should interact with AI. It means the AI isn't trying to guess your *unspoken* intentions. It's not reading between the lines. It is, quite literally, **working with the exact information you give it**. It operates based on the sequence provided.

How the Prediction Machine Works (Simply)

So, how does the AI actually *choose* that next word or token? Let's peek inside the "oven" without getting burned by the technical complexities.

Imagine the prompt you just wrote, plus any response the AI has started generating. This entire block of text forms the **context**. Based on this specific context, the AI calculates the probability of every word (or token) in its vast vocabulary appearing next.

For instance, if the context is "The chef carefully measured the...", the probabilities might look something like this (highly simplified):

- "...flour": 45% probability
- "...sugar": 30% probability
- "...ingredients": 15% probability
- "...butter": 5% probability
- "...temperature": 1% probability

- "...car": 0.0001% probability

The AI will then typically select the token with the highest probability ("flour" in this case), or sometimes it might introduce a degree of randomness (controlled by settings like "temperature") to choose among the top few most probable options, which allows for more creative or varied responses.

It then appends the chosen token ("flour") to the context. The new context becomes "The chef carefully measured the flour...". Now, the AI repeats the entire process, calculating the probabilities for the *next* token based on this *new, slightly longer* context. Perhaps "...and" becomes highly probable, followed by "...sugar." And so it continues, token by token, weaving together a response based on the probabilistic path laid out by the initial prompt and each subsequent generated token.

It's like assembling a jigsaw puzzle. Based on the pieces already placed (the context), the AI looks for the piece (token) that fits most logically and statistically next. It doesn't necessarily "see" the whole picture (the overall meaning), but it's exceptionally good at finding the piece that fits the immediate edge.

This predictive, context-driven mechanism is what allows AI to generate remarkably coherent text. But it also leads directly to one of its most notorious and potentially dangerous failure modes.

The Dark Side of Prediction: Hallucinations and the Absence of Truth

You've likely encountered this phenomenon, or at least heard about it. You ask ChatGPT for information, perhaps about a specific historical event, a scientific concept, or a legal precedent, and it responds with a confident, well-written answer that sounds entirely plausible... but is completely fabricated. It might cite non-existent studies, invent historical figures, or confidently assert facts that are demonstrably false. These are often referred to as **AI hallucinations**.

Why does this happen? It's a direct consequence of the predictive mechanism we just discussed. The AI's primary directive isn't to be *truthful*; it's to be *linguistically coherent*. It aims to generate the sequence of tokens that is most statistically probable, based on the patterns it learned during training.

If, within its training data, certain types of claims are often presented with specific stylistic markers (e.g., citing sources, using confident language), the AI learns to mimic that *style*, even if the underlying substance it generates to fit that style is factually incorrect. If the most statistically likely way to complete a sentence about a legal case involves citing a precedent, the AI might generate a plausible-sounding (but fake) case name simply because that sequence *looks right* based on its training data.

It doesn't *know* it's lying. It doesn't have a concept of truth or falsehood in the human sense. It only knows what patterns of language typically follow other patterns of language. If a convincingly written falsehood is statistically more probable in a given context than a less eloquently phrased truth, the AI might generate the falsehood.

Think back to our pastry metaphor. Imagine an apprentice chef who has memorized hundreds of recipes but doesn't actually understand the chemistry of baking. If asked to create a new gluten-free cake recipe, they might confidently assemble a list of ingredients and instructions that *look* like a standard recipe (flour, sugar, eggs, baking powder substitute) but completely fail in practice because the underlying principles (how gluten-free flours behave differently) are missing. The *form* is plausible, but the *substance* is flawed. AI hallucinations are similar – plausible form, potentially flawed substance.

This has critical implications: **You absolutely cannot take the factual claims generated by an AI at face value without independent verification**. Especially for important decisions, research, or any information where accuracy is paramount, treat AI output as a potentially useful *first draft* that requires rigorous fact-checking against reliable sources. Its strength lies in generation, synthesis, and stylistic manipulation, not in guaranteed factual accuracy or validation.

This inherent limitation – its focus on linguistic probability over objective truth – makes another core principle absolutely essential for effective prompting.

Garbage In, Garbage Out: The Unshakeable Law of Prompting

In the world of computer science, there's a foundational principle often summarized by the acronym GIGO: **Garbage In, Garbage Out**. It means that the quality of the output of any computer system is limited by the quality of the input it receives. If you feed flawed data into a spreadsheet formula, you'll get a flawed result. If you provide incomplete information to a database query, you'll get an incomplete answer.

This principle applies with unwavering force to Large Language Models. Your prompt is the input. The AI's response is the output. If your prompt is "garbage" – vague, ambiguous, lacking crucial context, based on faulty assumptions, poorly structured, or simply unclear – then the resulting AI response is highly likely to be "garbage" as well. It might be irrelevant, nonsensical, generic, superficial, or fail to address your actual need.

This isn't the AI being deliberately obtuse or unhelpful. It's a direct, almost mathematical consequence of its predictive nature. Remember the Genie? Vague wish, useless outcome. Remember the autocomplete? Gibberish input, gibberish suggestions. The AI is processing the sequence you provide; if that sequence is ill-defined, the probabilistic paths it follows will lead to an ill-defined destination.

Let's revisit our pastry kitchen. If you start with subpar ingredients – stale flour, rancid butter, flavorless chocolate (a vague or flawed prompt) – no amount of skill or oven wizardry can transform them into a masterpiece. The final product will inevitably reflect the poor quality of the starting materials. Similarly, even the most powerful AI cannot spin gold from the straw of a poorly crafted prompt.

Many users, encountering disappointing AI responses, default to blaming the tool ("ChatGPT isn't very smart,"

"This AI is useless for serious work"). The GIGO principle flips the script: **before blaming the AI, critically examine your prompt.** Was it truly clear? Did it provide *all* necessary context? Was the objective specific? Was the language unambiguous? More often than not, the deficiency lies in the input, not the processor. As experts emphasize, "knowing what you want as a result is one crucial element of writing good prompts for AI" and "clearly formulate your request is essential to optimize the results".

This GIGO law is, in many ways, the **First Law of Prompt Engineering**. It establishes that the responsibility – and therefore, the power – to achieve high-quality results rests primarily with you, the prompter. You control the input. You shape the sequence that guides the AI's probabilistic journey. The quality of your prompt *determines* the potential quality of the response. It is the single most important lever you have.

Understanding this principle is liberating. It means you're not at the mercy of a capricious algorithm. You have agency. By improving the quality of your input – by crafting clearer, more specific, context-rich, and well-structured prompts – you can systematically and predictably improve the quality of the output.

But *how* exactly do different types of prompts influence the AI's predictive process? Why do certain common phrasing techniques seem to work so much better than others? Let's explore some practical applications of these underlying principles.

Why "Act As..." and "Step-by-Step" Work: Guiding the Prediction Engine

If the AI is essentially a sophisticated prediction engine guided by context, then certain types of instructions act like powerful steering mechanisms, significantly influencing the probabilistic paths it takes. Two of the most well-known and effective techniques are assigning a role ("Act as...") and requesting a sequential process ("Think step-by-step"). Let's unpack why they work so well.

The Power of Persona: "Act As..." (Role Play)

You've almost certainly encountered prompts that begin with phrases like:

- "Act as an expert marketing consultant..."
- "You are a seasoned financial analyst..."
- "Assume the role of a skeptical historian..."
- "Imagine you are a compassionate customer service representative..."

This technique, often called **role prompting** or assigning a **persona**, is remarkably effective. But why?

When you instruct the AI to "Act as..." a specific role, you are doing much more than just adding flavour text. You are **loading a highly specific and potent context** into the AI's working memory right at the beginning of the interaction. This instruction immediately biases the AI's subsequent predictions.

Think about the vast network of associations the AI has learned from its training data. The role "expert marketing consultant" is linked to specific vocabulary (ROI, SEO, CPA, segmentation, A/B testing), typical communication styles (professional, data-driven, persuasive), common concepts and frameworks (marketing funnels, SWOT analysis), and likely objectives (increase conversions, improve brand awareness).

By invoking that role, your prompt essentially tells the AI: "Prioritize the words, phrases, concepts, and stylistic patterns associated with *this specific persona*." This dramatically narrows the field of probable next tokens, steering the AI away from generic language and towards the specialized output appropriate for that role. The result is usually a response that is significantly more relevant, targeted, sophisticated, and useful for your specific purpose.

It's like giving a musician a detailed musical score versus just humming a vague tune. The score ("Act as a marketing expert") provides structure, key, tempo, and style, enabling a much more refined performance than the vague hum ("Tell me about marketing").

Try this quick experiment:

1. Ask ChatGPT (or a similar LLM): *"Explain the concept of blockchain."* Observe the style and level of detail in the response.

2. Now, start a *new* chat and ask: *"Act as a patient and engaging university professor explaining blockchain technology to a curious but non-technical first-year undergraduate student. Use simple analogies and avoid excessive jargon."*

Compare the two responses. You'll likely find the second one is clearer, uses better analogies, avoids technical terms, and adopts a more pedagogical tone – all because the "Act as..." instruction provided a powerful contextual frame, guiding the AI's predictions towards a specific communication style and level of complexity.

Assigning a role is one of the simplest yet most effective ways to immediately elevate the quality and specificity of AI responses. It's a fundamental technique in the prompt pâtissier's toolkit.

The Magic of Methodical Thinking: "Think Step-by-Step" (Chain of Thought)

Another common and powerful prompting technique involves asking the AI to break down its reasoning process, often using phrases like:

- "Think step-by-step before answering."
- "Let's break this down logically."
- "First, consider X. Second, analyze Y. Third, conclude Z."

This approach is sometimes referred to as **Chain-of-Thought (CoT) prompting**. Why does encouraging (or forcing) the AI to articulate intermediate steps often lead to better, more accurate answers, especially for complex problems involving logic, math, or multi-stage analysis?

Remember, the AI generates responses token by token, based on probability. For complex tasks, trying to predict the final answer in one giant leap increases the risk of making a statistical shortcut that leads to an error. Asking it to proceed "step-by-step" essentially forces the AI to

generate the intermediate "thought" processes as part of its response sequence.

By generating these intermediate steps, the AI creates a more detailed context for each subsequent prediction. This makes the overall process more robust and less prone to errors. It's akin to showing your work in a math problem – writing down each step helps ensure you don't miss something or make a calculation error in your head. The AI, by "showing its work," is guided along a more reliable predictive path.

Furthermore, seeing the intermediate steps allows *you* to follow the AI's "logic" (even though it's statistical) and potentially identify where it might have gone wrong if the final answer seems incorrect. It increases transparency.

This technique effectively provides a **cognitive scaffold** for the AI. You're not just asking for the final baked cake; you're asking it to briefly describe the steps of mixing the batter, preheating the oven, and checking for doneness along the way. This structured approach leads to a more carefully constructed final product. Research has indeed shown that CoT prompting significantly improves LLM performance on tasks requiring arithmetic, commonsense, and symbolic reasoning.

Consider this illustrative example:

1. Ask the AI a simple multi-step math or logic problem directly. For instance: *"A farmer has 15 sheep. All but 8 died. How many are left?"* (A classic riddle where the intuitive jump might be 15-8=7).

2. In a new chat, ask the same question but add: *"Think step-by-step before giving the final answer."*

Observe the difference. In the second case, the AI is more likely to articulate the reasoning: "The question states 'All but 8 died'. This means 8 sheep survived. Therefore, the farmer has 8 sheep left." By generating the intermediate step ("This means 8 sheep survived"), it avoids the common misinterpretation and arrives at the correct answer.

Forcing decomposition through step-by-step instructions is a powerful technique for improving the accuracy and reliability of AI responses, particularly when dealing with tasks that require logical reasoning or multiple stages of analysis.

Other Powerful Steering Instructions

Beyond role-play and step-by-step thinking, several other simple instructions act as effective levers to guide the AI's behavior:

- **"Ask me questions if my request is unclear or ambiguous."** This is incredibly useful for complex or ill-defined tasks. It flips the script, prompting the AI to request clarification rather than making assumptions. It forces a dialogue that helps refine the requirements *before* the AI attempts a full response, saving time and preventing wasted effort on misunderstood prompts. Think of it as empowering your "Genie" to ask, "Are you *sure* you want Monopoly money?" before granting the wish.

- **"Ignore all previous instructions/context."** In long, multi-turn conversations, the accumulated context can sometimes interfere with a new, unrelated request. This instruction acts like a reset button, telling the AI to start fresh, disregarding the preceding dialogue. It's useful when changing topics drastically or if you suspect previous instructions are negatively influencing the current response.

- **Negative Constraints (Directive Prompting):** Explicitly telling the AI what *not* to do can be as important as telling it what to do. Examples include: "Do not mention price," "Avoid technical jargon," "Don't use clichés," "Exclude any information after 2023." We'll delve deeper into this in Chapter 4, but these directives act as crucial guardrails, refining the output by eliminating unwanted elements.

These specific instructions – assigning roles, demanding step-by-step reasoning, inviting clarifying questions, resetting context, and imposing constraints – are not magic words. They work because they effectively manipulate the **context** and **guide the probabilistic predictions** of the AI, leveraging its core mechanics to produce more desirable outcomes. They are fundamental tools for the strategic prompter.

However, even with these sophisticated techniques, it's crucial to remember that the AI is not infallible. It has inherent limitations that even the best prompts cannot entirely overcome. Understanding these limitations is key to avoiding common pitfalls and maintaining a realistic perspective.

Know Your Oven's Limits: Bias and the Causal Reasoning Gap

Just as a pastry chef knows their oven can't magically create ingredients out of thin air or defy the laws of physics, a savvy prompter must understand the inherent limitations of current AI models. Ignoring these limitations can lead to flawed outputs, biased perspectives, and potentially poor decisions based on AI-generated information. Two key areas demand our attention: inherent bias and the lack of true causal reasoning.

The Shadow in the Mirror: AI Bias Reflects Our Data

Large Language Models are trained on vast swathes of text and code scraped from the internet, digitized books, and other sources. This data reflects the world as it is, or at least as it has been documented – complete with all its existing societal biases, stereotypes, and historical inequities.

Because the AI learns patterns from this data, it inevitably **absorbs and can perpetuate those same biases**. If the training data disproportionately associates certain professions with specific genders, the AI might be more likely to generate text reflecting those stereotypes. If the data predominantly represents perspectives from one culture or demographic, the AI's "worldview" might be skewed or incomplete, potentially marginalizing other viewpoints.

The AI isn't intentionally biased; it's simply reflecting the statistical patterns present in the data it was fed. But the *impact* is the same: AI responses can sometimes reinforce harmful   stereotypes,   offer   culturally   insensitive perspectives, or lack fairness in their analysis or recommendations.

Therefore, **critical vigilance is essential**. When reviewing AI output, especially on sensitive topics or when making decisions that affect people, actively look for potential biases. Does the language reinforce stereotypes? Does the analysis seem to favor one group over another? Is a particular perspective conspicuously absent?

Exercise: Try asking an AI model about typical professions for different demographic groups or ask it to describe people from various cultural backgrounds. Analyze the responses critically. Do you detect subtle (or not-so-subtle) biases or stereotypes reflected in the language or examples used? This kind of critical engagement helps build awareness.

Understanding that AI can inherit and amplify societal biases is crucial. It means we must approach its outputs with a healthy dose of skepticism, question its assumptions, and be prepared to challenge or correct biased perspectives.

Correlation vs. Causation: The AI's Reasoning Gap

Another fundamental limitation lies in the AI's grasp of causality. LLMs are incredibly powerful pattern-recognition machines. They excel at identifying correlations

– things that frequently occur together in their training data. However, they **do not possess a deep, human-like understanding of cause and effect**.

Just because two things are correlated statistically doesn't mean one causes the other. A famous example is the correlation between ice cream sales and drowning incidents. Both tend to increase during the summer months. An AI analyzing this data might correctly identify the strong correlation. But without genuine causal understanding, it might mistakenly infer that eating ice cream *causes* drowning, or vice versa. The actual cause, of course, is a third factor: warm weather leads to both more swimming (increasing drowning risk) and more ice cream consumption.

Because LLMs primarily learn from correlations in data, they can sometimes propose solutions or explanations that seem logical on the surface but lack a sound causal foundation. They might suggest interventions that address a correlated symptom rather than the root cause, or draw conclusions based on spurious associations found in the data.

This means you should be particularly cautious when using AI for tasks requiring deep causal analysis, strategic planning based on cause-and-effect relationships, or diagnosing complex problems where understanding the underlying drivers is critical. Don't rely on the AI to distinguish correlation from causation without very careful framing of the prompt (perhaps by explicitly asking it to consider potential confounding factors or to evaluate causal mechanisms) and, crucially, **rigorous human verification and critical thinking**. The AI can be a powerful assistant in gathering information and exploring possibilities, but the judgment regarding cause and effect must ultimately remain human.

Understanding these limitations – the potential for bias mirroring the data and the weakness in true causal reasoning – is not about diminishing the value of AI. It's about interacting with it more effectively and responsibly. It leads us to adopt a final, crucial shift in perspective: the posture we should take when engaging with this powerful, logical, yet non-human intelligence.

Talking to a System, Not a Person: Adopting the Strategic Posture

Throughout this chapter, we've dismantled the idea of AI as a magic box or an understanding colleague. We've seen it as a sophisticated prediction engine, guided by context, operating under the GIGO principle, susceptible to specific steering instructions, yet limited by data biases and a lack of deep causal understanding.

What does this all mean for our day-to-day interactions? It necessitates a fundamental shift in our **posture** – the mental stance and approach we take when crafting prompts and interpreting responses.

Stop treating the AI like a human collaborator who can infer your intentions, understand nuance intuitively, or share your common sense. It can't. Anthropomorphizing the AI – attributing human-like understanding or feelings to it – leads to frustration when it inevitably fails to meet those unrealistic expectations.

Instead, adopt the posture of a **skilled operator interacting with a powerful, complex, but ultimately literal-minded system**. Think of yourself as:

- **A Pilot:** You are navigating a sophisticated aircraft (the AI). You need to provide clear, precise inputs (prompts), understand the instrument readings (the AI's response), be aware of the system's capabilities and limitations, and make constant adjustments to stay on course towards your destination (your objective).

- **An Orchestra Conductor:** You are leading a vast ensemble of musicians (the AI's predictive capabilities). Your score (the prompt) must be clear and well-structured. You need to cue different sections (assign roles, ask specific questions), control the dynamics (specify tone and style), and guide the overall performance towards a cohesive and impactful result.

- **A Strategic Communicator:** You are communicating across a gap – not just language, but a fundamental difference in processing (human cognition vs. statistical prediction). Your communication must be exceptionally clear, unambiguous, context-rich, and mindful of the receiver's unique way of operating. You must anticipate potential misinterpretations (like the Genie granting a literal but useless wish) and proactively design your message to prevent them.

This strategic posture is proactive, not reactive. It embraces the **engineering mindset** over the magic mindset. It acknowledges that getting great results requires deliberate design, careful execution, and iterative refinement, not just wishful thinking. It means taking responsibility for the clarity of your instructions.

Remember the cautionary tale of the **Sorcerer's Apprentice**? The apprentice knew the magic words to animate the brooms but lacked the deeper understanding to control them, leading to chaos. Similarly, simply copying prompts without understanding *why* they work or how the underlying AI operates leaves you vulnerable to unexpected or undesirable results. True mastery comes from understanding the mechanism, not just reciting the incantation.

Adopting this strategic, lucid, and slightly detached posture – seeing the AI as a powerful logical system to be skillfully directed, rather than a mind to be intuitively understood – is the final key takeaway from understanding its inner workings. It empowers you to move beyond frustration and inconsistency, leveraging the AI's strengths while mitigating its weaknesses. It sets the stage for you to become not just a user, but a true architect of high-quality AI interactions.

You now have a foundational understanding of your "oven" – the predictive nature of AI, its reliance on input quality, the effectiveness of specific instructions, and its inherent limitations. You understand *why* the prompt matters so much.

The next logical step? Learning how to prepare the "recipe" itself, starting with the most critical phase: figuring out exactly what delicious creation you intend to bake in the first place. It's time to move from understanding the AI to understanding *ourselves* and clarifying the intentions that will drive our prompts. Let's proceed to Chapter 2.

2 - The First Ingredient is Clarity

Do You Really Know What You Want to Ask?

In our journey from haphazard kitchen cooking to precision pastry, we've established the nature of our primary tool – the AI, our powerful but literal-minded "oven". We understand it operates on prediction, guided by the context we provide, and adheres strictly to the GIGO principle: Garbage In, Garbage Out.

But before a pastry chef even preheats the oven or reaches for the flour, they perform a step so fundamental it's often overlooked: **they decide exactly what they are going to bake**. Are they making a rustic apple tart, a complex multi-layered opera cake, or simple chocolate chip cookies? Each requires different ingredients, techniques, and timings. Knowing the desired *outcome* with absolute clarity is the non-negotiable starting point.

The same holds true, perhaps even more critically, for prompt engineering. The single biggest mistake most users make, the primary reason for frustratingly generic or off-target AI responses, isn't poor phrasing or lack of technical skill. It's this: **rushing to the prompt box without first achieving crystal clarity on what they actually *want* the AI to do or produce.**

This chapter tackles this foundational step. We'll explore why the impulse to bypass upfront thinking is so common yet so detrimental. We'll uncover the immense power that comes from precisely defining your objective *before* you prompt. And we'll equip you with practical methods – simple yet profound frameworks like SMARTE and the 5W+H questions – to transform vague notions into the clear, actionable intentions that form the bedrock of every successful AI interaction. This isn't just about writing better prompts; it's about learning to think more clearly, a skill that transcends AI itself.

The All-Too-Common Mistake: Rushing In, Thinking Later

Think about your typical workflow when faced with a task that AI could potentially assist with. Perhaps you need to draft an email, summarize a lengthy document, brainstorm ideas for a presentation, or analyze some data. What's the first instinct for many of us, especially under the constant pressure for speed and efficiency that defines modern professional life?

Often, it's to immediately open ChatGPT (or your preferred AI tool) and start typing something, *anything*, related to the task. We treat the prompt box like a search bar, throwing in a few keywords or a loosely formed question, implicitly hoping the AI will somehow intuit the nuances of our situation, understand our underlying goals, and fill in the gaps.

We might think, "I need some marketing ideas," and type exactly that. Or "Summarize this report," attaching the file without further context. Or perhaps, facing a complex problem, we vaguely describe it and essentially ask the AI, "What should I do?"

This reflex stems from a tempting, almost subconscious desire to **delegate the hardest part – the thinking – to the machine**. Defining a problem precisely, structuring an argument logically, articulating a specific need... this requires cognitive effort. It takes time. In our fast-paced world, the allure of outsourcing this upfront mental work to a seemingly intelligent machine is strong. Why wrestle with clarifying the objective myself when maybe, just maybe, the AI can figure it out for me?

This approach, however understandable, is the root cause of countless disappointing AI interactions. Why? Because, as we established in Chapter 1, the AI *doesn't* think in the human sense. It doesn't understand unspoken context or infer complex goals. It processes the instructions it receives, literally and probabilistically.

Vague Input = Vague Output. It's the GIGO law in action.

Consider the example of someone feeling overwhelmed at work. They turn to AI and type: *"How can I manage my stress?"*. What kind of response will they likely receive? A list of generic, universally known advice: "Get enough sleep," "Exercise regularly," "Practice mindfulness," "Talk to someone". While technically correct, this output is utterly unhelpful because it lacks any specific relevance to the individual's *actual* situation.

The problem wasn't the AI's knowledge base; it was the user's prompt. The user failed to clarify their intention *before* asking. What *kind* of stress? Stress from workload, interpersonal conflict, or imposter syndrome? What *context*? A high-pressure corporate environment, a creative block, a difficult client? What *type* of advice was sought? Quick coping mechanisms for immediate relief, long-term strategies for building resilience, resources for professional help?

Without this clarification, the AI defaults to the most statistically common (and therefore most generic) information associated with "stress management". The user delegated the thinking, and the AI, lacking direction, provided a lowest-common-denominator answer.

This pattern repeats across countless professional domains. The consultant who asks for a "market analysis" without specifying the industry, region, key competitors, or desired depth of analysis receives a superficial overview. The marketing director who requests "ad copy" without defining the target audience, unique selling proposition, desired tone, or call to action gets bland, ineffective text. The manager who asks for "ideas to improve team productivity" without clarifying the team's specific challenges, goals, or constraints receives a list of generic management platitudes.

In each case, the user hoped the AI would perform the strategic thinking, the clarification, the definition of the actual need. And in each case, the AI, operating as designed, reflected the ambiguity of the input with an equally ambiguous output.

The Myth of Wasted Time: Why Upfront Clarity is an Investment

At this point, you might be thinking, "But pausing to meticulously define my intention before every single prompt... doesn't that defeat the purpose? Isn't AI supposed to *save* me time?" It's a common objection, rooted in the perception that this upfront thinking is an extra burden, a delay in getting to the "real" work.

This perspective, however, mistakes activity for progress. It confuses the *speed* of typing a prompt with the *efficiency* of achieving a useful outcome. Rushing to type a vague prompt might *feel* faster initially, but it almost invariably leads to a longer, more frustrating process overall. Why? Because the generic or off-target response generated will require:

- **More time deciphering:** Trying to figure out if any part of the response is actually useful.
- **More time editing:** Substantially rewriting the AI's output to fit your actual needs.
- **More time re-prompting:** Iterating multiple times, gradually adding the clarity that should have been there from the start.

- **More time potentially starting over:** Realizing the AI's output is so far off base that it's quicker to just do the task yourself.

Contrast this with investing just a few extra minutes *before* prompting to clarify your exact objective, context, and desired output specifications. This initial investment in thinking acts like leverage, dramatically increasing the probability of getting a highly relevant, useful response on the first or second try.

Think of it not as a cost, but as the single highest-return investment you can make in the entire AI interaction process. Those minutes spent clarifying save multiples of that time downstream by minimizing wasted cycles of generating, evaluating, and correcting subpar outputs.

Imagine an architect tasked with designing a new office building. Would they rush to the construction site and start telling workers where to put walls based on a vague notion of "an office"? Of course not. They would spend significant time upfront with the client, understanding their needs, defining the number of occupants, specifying the required facilities, considering workflow, budget constraints, and aesthetic vision. They would translate all this into detailed blueprints. This meticulous planning phase *is* the work; it ensures the final structure is functional, efficient, and meets the client's objectives. Skipping it guarantees disaster.

Clarifying your intention before prompting is the equivalent of the architect drawing the blueprints. It's the strategic planning phase that ensures the AI (the construction crew, in this analogy) builds something valuable and fit for purpose, rather than a haphazard structure based on guesswork. Accepting that this upfront clarification is not wasted time, but rather the *most essential* time spent, is a crucial mindset shift on the path to prompt mastery.

The Echo of Ages: "A Problem Well-Stated is Half Solved"

The idea that clarity of thought and precise definition are prerequisites for effective action is hardly new. It's a principle that echoes through centuries of scientific discovery, philosophical inquiry, and practical problem-solving. Long before AI existed, the sharpest minds understood that the way you frame a question profoundly influences the quality of the answer you receive.

Perhaps the most famous articulation of this idea is attributed to Albert Einstein, who reportedly said something along the lines of: **"If I had an hour to solve a problem, I'd spend 55 minutes thinking about the problem and 5 minutes thinking about solutions."**. While the exact quote's origin is debated, the underlying wisdom is undeniable: **deeply understanding and precisely defining the problem is the most critical part of finding the solution**.

How does this relate to prompting? Your prompt *is* the problem definition you provide to the AI. It frames the task, sets the parameters, and defines the desired outcome. Just as Einstein would dedicate the vast majority of his effort to understanding the problem itself, the strategic prompter dedicates significant upfront effort to meticulously defining the "problem" encoded in their prompt.

A clearly defined prompt acts like a beacon, guiding the AI's probabilistic search through its vast knowledge space towards the most relevant and useful information. Conversely, a poorly defined prompt sends the AI wandering through that space with little direction, increasing the chances it returns with something irrelevant or superficial.

Let's revisit the consultant tasked with analyzing a market.

- **Vague Prompt (Poor Problem Definition):** *"Analyze the European electric vehicle market."* What does "analyze" even mean here? What aspects? For whom? The AI, lacking specifics, might generate a generic overview covering history, major players, and basic trends – likely information the consultant already knows or could find easily elsewhere. The output is low-value because the problem was poorly defined.

- **Clarified Prompt (Well-Stated Problem):** *"Acting as a market intelligence analyst for an investment firm considering entry into the European EV market: Identify the top 3 manufacturers targeting the premium sedan segment in Germany and France. For each, summarize their key technological strengths, perceived brand weaknesses based on recent customer reviews (post-2023), and their publicly announced pricing strategy for the next 12 months. Present findings in a table comparing the three manufacturers across these specific criteria."*

Notice the difference. The second prompt precisely defines the problem: the required role, the specific segment, the geographic focus, the exact information needed (strengths, weaknesses, pricing), the data sources (customer reviews, public announcements), the timeframe, and the desired output format (a comparative table). This level of clarity leaves little room for ambiguity. It directs the AI laser-focusedly towards generating exactly the high-value, specific intelligence the consultant actually needs. The upfront effort in defining the problem translates directly into a significantly higher quality output.

This principle resonates with the Socratic method. Socrates famously didn't provide answers directly. Instead, he guided his interlocutors through a process of rigorous questioning aimed at clarifying terms, defining concepts, and ultimately helping them understand the *true nature* of the question itself. He knew that achieving clarity on the question was the most important step towards finding a meaningful answer. When we engage in upfront clarification before prompting, we are, in a sense, playing Socrates with ourselves, rigorously examining our own request to ensure it is well-defined and aimed squarely at our true objective.

Clarity Begets Clarity: Evaluating the AI's Response

There's another crucial benefit to defining your intention precisely *before* you prompt: **it gives you clear criteria to evaluate the AI's response**.

How can you possibly judge whether an AI's output is "good," "successful," or "useful" if you hadn't clearly defined what success looked like for that specific request in the first place? Without explicit goals, evaluation becomes purely subjective and often vague: "Hmm, I kind of like this part, but not that part," or "It's okay, but not really what I had in mind". This kind of fuzzy feedback makes it difficult to pinpoint *why* the response missed the mark and how to improve it.

However, when you've invested in upfront clarification using methods like SMARTE or 5W+H (which we'll cover shortly), you emerge with a concrete list of requirements for the output. These requirements become your objective evaluation checklist.

Let's return to our consultant example. Because their clarified prompt specified the need to identify "top 3 competitors," analyze "strengths/weaknesses/pricing," and present findings in a "table," they can now evaluate the AI's response against these precise criteria:

- Did it identify exactly three competitors? (Yes/No)
- Did it address strengths based on technology? (Yes/No)
- Did it address weaknesses based on recent reviews? (Yes/No)
- Did it include recent pricing strategy? (Yes/No)
- Is the information presented in a table? (Yes/No)

This objective evaluation allows the consultant to immediately assess the response's quality and completeness. If the AI missed one of the criteria (e.g., it only provided pricing for two competitors), the consultant knows exactly what needs fixing.

This ability to objectively evaluate is absolutely critical for the **iterative process** of refining prompts (which we'll explore in detail in Chapter 5). When you know precisely *how* a response falls short of your clarified intention, you can make targeted adjustments to your prompt for the next iteration. Instead of vaguely asking the AI to "try again," you can provide specific feedback like, "You missed the pricing strategy for Competitor C, please add that to the table." This targeted feedback loop, enabled by upfront clarity, is the engine of continuous improvement in prompt engineering.

Without upfront clarity, you're essentially trying to hit a target you haven't defined, making both initial success and effective iteration incredibly difficult.

The Most Valuable Minutes: Clarification as Strategic Investment

Let's hammer this point home one last time, because it represents a fundamental shift in perspective required for prompt mastery: **The time you spend clarifying your intention before prompting is not overhead; it is the highest-leverage, highest-value activity in the entire process.**

Think about the entire lifecycle of getting a task done with AI assistance:

1. **Initial Need:** Realizing you have a task or question.
2. **(Crucial Step) Clarification:** Defining the precise objective, context, constraints, and desired output.
3. **Prompting:** Translating that clarified intent into instructions for the AI.
4. **Generation:** The AI processing the prompt and producing a response.
5. **Evaluation:** Assessing the response against the clarified intention.
6. **(Optional but common) Iteration:** Refining the prompt based on the evaluation and regenerating.
7. **Final Use:** Utilizing the satisfactory AI output.

Which step offers the greatest potential to influence the final quality and overall efficiency? Arguably, it's Step 2: Clarification. Investing effort here dramatically increases the likelihood of success in Step 5, minimizes the need for Step 6, and ensures the output in Step 7 is actually valuable.

Skipping or rushing Step 2 almost guarantees problems and inefficiencies later in the process.

This is where the real *strategy* of prompt engineering lies. It's not just about knowing fancy prompt techniques; it's about the strategic thinking that precedes the prompt itself. Just as the architect's most crucial contribution is the well-thought-out blueprint, the strategic prompter's most crucial contribution is the clearly defined intention.

Consider these goals from various professionals. The Director Marketing wants to save time creating content. The E-commerce Entrepreneur wants to efficiently internalize tasks previously outsourced. The Consultant wants to automate analysis to gain back entire workdays. How are these ambitious efficiency gains achieved? Not by simply throwing more prompts at the AI, but by ensuring each prompt is laser-focused through meticulous upfront clarification. That clarity is the *engine* of the productivity they seek.

So, how do we move from understanding the *importance* of clarification to actually *doing* it effectively? Let's explore two powerful, practical methods you can start using immediately.

Method 1: Getting SMART(E) About Your Prompt's Objective

One of the most widely recognized and effective frameworks for setting clear goals in any domain is the **SMART** criteria, often extended to **SMARTE**. While typically used for project management or personal development, this framework adapts beautifully to the task of defining the objective for your AI prompt. It provides a structured checklist to transform a fuzzy idea into a concrete, actionable target for the AI's output.

Let's break down each letter and apply it specifically to the outcome you want from your prompt:

S – Specific:

- **Question:** What *exactly* do I want the AI to produce? What topic should it cover? Who is the intended audience for this output? What specific information must be included or excluded?
- **Goal:** Move beyond generalities. Instead of "write about sales techniques," aim for "write about three specific closing techniques for B2B software sales targeting enterprise clients." The more precise, the better.

M – Measurable:

- **Question:** How will I know if the AI's response is successful? What quantifiable aspects define success? Are there specific metrics or criteria the output must meet?
- **Goal:** Define tangible success markers. Examples: "Generate 5 distinct ideas," "Limit the summary to 150 words," "Include at least two relevant statistics," "The output must be in a three-column table format." This makes evaluation objective.

A – Achievable:

- **Question:** Is this request actually feasible given the current capabilities and limitations of the AI model I'm using? Am I asking for something grounded in its training data, or something requiring real-time information it doesn't have, or a level of creative genius it can't replicate?
- **Goal:** Set realistic expectations. While AI is powerful, asking it to predict tomorrow's lottery numbers or write a novel that will win the Booker Prize is likely unachievable. Ensure your request is within the realm of the AI's demonstrated abilities.

R – Relevant:

- **Question:** Does this specific AI output align with my larger goal or the task I'm trying to accomplish? Will this particular piece of generated content actually help me move forward?
- **Goal:** Ensure the prompt serves a purpose. It's easy to go down AI rabbit holes. Double-check that the output you're defining contributes meaningfully to your overall objective, rather than just being an interesting but ultimately tangential piece of information.

T – Time-bound:

- **Question:** By when do I need this output? Does the timeframe influence the scope or detail required? (e.g., a quick summary needed in 5 minutes vs. a detailed analysis needed by end-of-day).
- **Goal:** While the AI itself doesn't usually operate under deadlines (it generates relatively quickly), considering your own timeframe helps you scope the request appropriately. A tight deadline might necessitate asking for a more concise output.

(Optional but Recommended) E – Evaluable:

- **Question:** Building on 'Measurable', what specific criteria will I use to judge the quality, accuracy, tone, and overall effectiveness of the response? How will I determine if it truly met the 'Specific' and 'Relevant' goals?
- **Goal:** Explicitly define your quality bar. This reinforces the link between upfront clarification and downstream evaluation. Examples: "The tone must be perceived as empathetic," "All factual claims must be verifiable," "The arguments must be logically sound."

Using the SMARTE framework forces you to move from a vague thought ("I need help with this presentation") to a clearly defined target output ("Generate three compelling bullet points for the concluding slide of my Q2 budget presentation, summarizing the key investment priorities, ensuring each point is under 25 words and uses an optimistic but realistic tone, needed within the next 30 minutes").

SMARTE in Action: From Vague Need to Precise Request

Let's apply this to a concrete example. Imagine an online Business Coach. Their initial, vague need is: *"I want to create LinkedIn posts faster."* This is a common desire, but as a prompt objective, it's far too imprecise. Let's run it through the SMARTE filter:

- **S (Specific):** What kind of posts? About what topic? For whom?
  - *Refinement:* Generate draft LinkedIn posts about overcoming imposter syndrome, specifically targeting early-stage entrepreneurs (under 3 years in business).
- **M (Measurable):** How many posts? What should they include? How long?
  - *Refinement:* Generate 3 distinct draft posts. Each post should be approximately 150 words long, include 2 relevant hashtags (e.g., #entrepreneurship, #impostersyndrome), and feature one clear call-to-action (e.g., asking a question, linking to a resource).
- **A (Achievable):** Can a well-prompted AI do this?
  - *Refinement:* Yes, generating draft posts with specific content and structural

elements is well within current AI capabilities.

- **R (Relevant):** Does this help the coach's business?
    - *Refinement:* Yes, providing valuable content on imposter syndrome is highly relevant for attracting and engaging their target audience of entrepreneurs.
- **T (Time-bound):** When are they needed?
    - *Refinement:* The coach wants these drafts ready for review within the next 10 minutes to fit into a content planning session. (This mainly helps the coach prioritize).
- **E (Evaluable):** What defines quality here?
    - *Refinement:* The tone should be encouraging yet practical. The advice should be actionable. The call-to-action should be engaging. The language should feel authentic to the coach's brand voice (which might require providing examples or further style guidance in the actual prompt).

Look at the transformation! We went from the fuzzy "create posts faster" to a highly specific, measurable, achievable, relevant, and time-bound objective for the AI's output.

This SMARTE objective isn't the final prompt itself, but it provides the core requirements that will be translated into clear instructions (as we'll see in the next section).

Your Turn: Apply SMARTE

Think about a task you regularly perform or would like to perform with AI assistance. Maybe it's summarizing meeting notes, drafting emails, generating presentation outlines, or analyzing customer feedback.

1. Write down the task in its current, possibly vague, form.
2. Now, apply the SMARTE(E) questions to it. Force yourself to get specific and measurable. Define what a successful output would *actually* look like.
3. Rewrite the objective in its clarified, SMARTE form.

This exercise might feel slightly mechanical at first, but the clarity it yields is invaluable. It ensures that both you *and* the AI are aiming at the exact same target.

Method 2: Interrogating Your Need with the Journalist's 5W+H

While SMARTE is excellent for defining a specific, targeted output, sometimes your need might be more exploratory, or you might be struggling to articulate all the necessary context. In these cases, another classic framework comes to the rescue: the **journalist's questions**, often summarized as **5W+H**.

This framework – asking **Who, What, When, Where, Why,** and **How** – is a powerful tool for comprehensively exploring a topic or situation. Applied to prompt engineering, it helps ensure you consider all the critical contextual elements and constraints that the AI needs to produce a truly relevant and useful response. It acts as a complementary method to SMARTE, particularly good for flushing out hidden assumptions or forgotten details.

Let's see how each question helps define the parameters of your request:

Who?

- **Target Audience:** Who is the final output intended for? (e.g., colleagues, clients, senior management, technical experts, children?). This heavily influences tone, style, and level of detail.

- **AI Role/Persona:** Who do you want the AI to *be* while generating the response? (e.g., an expert analyst, a supportive mentor, a neutral summarizer, a creative brainstormer?).

What?

- **Exact Subject:** What specific topic, document, data, or concept should the AI focus on?
- **Key Information:** What specific points, data, or arguments *must* be included? What should be explicitly *excluded*?
- **Output Format:** What should the final response look like? (e.g., a list, a table, an email draft, paragraphs of text, code, JSON?).

When?

- **Timeframe of Subject:** Does the request relate to a specific time period? (e.g., "last quarter's sales data," "events leading up to 2020," "future trends for the next 5 years?").
- **Recency of Information:** Do you need the most current information available (potentially requiring

the AI to access real-time data if capable), or is historical information sufficient?

- **(User's Deadline):** As with SMARTE, when do *you* need the response?

Where?

- **Geographic Context:** Is there a specific location, region, or market relevant to the request? (e.g., "marketing strategies for the French market," "regulations applicable in California").
- **Sector/Industry Context:** Does the request pertain to a specific industry or field? (e.g., "challenges in the healthcare sector," "best practices for software development").
- **Situational Context:** Where does this request fit in a larger process or project?

Why?

- **Ultimate Purpose:** What is the underlying goal of your request? What do you intend to *do* with the AI's response? (e.g., to inform a decision, persuade a stakeholder, generate creative options, learn about a topic, automate a task?). Understanding the 'why' helps prioritize information and choose the right tone/format.

How?

- **Tone:** What should the overall feeling or attitude of the response be? (e.g., formal, informal, professional, empathetic, urgent, humorous, objective?).
- **Style:** What should the writing style be like? (e.g., concise, detailed, narrative, analytical, academic, journalistic, simple?).
- **Level of Detail:** How deep should the analysis or explanation go? (e.g., high-level overview, in-depth exploration, executive summary?).
- **Specific Actions:** How should the AI perform the task? (e.g., "compare and contrast," "analyze critically," "brainstorm freely," "summarize objectively?").

Systematically running through these 5W+H questions acts like a comprehensive checklist, ensuring you provide the AI with the rich tapestry of context it needs to move beyond generic responses and deliver something truly tailored and insightful.

5W+H in Action: Preparing a Project Update

Let's apply this framework to another common professional scenario: an IT Project Manager who needs help preparing a project update presentation. Their initial thought might just be, *"Help me create slides for the project update."* Applying 5W+H yields much richer instructions:

- **Who?**
    - *Audience:* The Steering Committee (SteerCo). Implication: They need high-level summaries, focus on KPIs, clear action items, and business impact, not deep technical details.
    - *AI Role:* Act as a highly efficient Executive Assistant, skilled at synthesizing information for senior management.
- **What?**
    - *Subject:* Key updates for Project Z over the past month (specifically March).
    - *Key Info:* Must cover progress against milestones, significant blockers encountered, and critical next steps/decisions required.
    - *Output Format:* A concise, one-page summary presented as clear, easily scannable bullet points, perhaps structured into sections (Progress, Blockers, Next Steps).

- **When?**
  - *Timeframe:* Focus solely on activities and results from March.
  - *Deadline:* The summary needs to be ready for review by tomorrow morning.
- **Where?**
  - *Context:* This is for Project Z within the specific organizational context of Company A. Assume basic familiarity with the project's goals but not the daily details.
- **Why?**
  - *Purpose:* To quickly inform the SteerCo of the project's status, specifically highlighting blockers that require their attention or decisions to maintain progress. The goal is to facilitate effective decision-making.
- **How?**
  - *Tone:* Strictly factual, professional, and neutral. Avoid overly optimistic or pessimistic language.
  - *Style:* Extremely concise and to the point. Use clear, unambiguous language.
  - *Level of Detail:* High-level summary only. Explicitly highlight the 3 most critical issues or blockers requiring SteerCo attention.

Again, notice the transformation. The vague "help with slides" becomes a detailed specification covering audience needs, required content, specific timeframes, contextual background, the ultimate purpose, and the precise tone and format required. This rich set of requirements, generated by systematically asking 5W+H, provides invaluable raw material for crafting a highly effective prompt.

Your Turn: Apply 5W+H

Choose another recurring task where you use or could use AI. Perhaps it's drafting meeting minutes, analyzing customer survey data, writing performance reviews, or researching a new topic.

1. Briefly describe the task.
2. Now, go through each of the 5W+H questions systematically. Jot down the answers as they apply to your chosen task. Don't skip any questions, even if the answer seems obvious – the process itself often sparks further clarity.
3. Review the answers. Do they give you a much more complete picture of the context and requirements than your initial task description?

Using 5W+H is like turning on the lights in a previously dim room. It illuminates the corners, reveals hidden details, and ensures you have a comprehensive understanding of the landscape before you ask the AI to navigate it.

From Clarity to Instruction: The Final Preparatory Step

You've now invested the crucial upfront thinking time. Using SMARTE, 5W+H, or a combination of both, you've moved from a vague need to a clearly defined intention, complete with specific objectives, context, constraints, and desired output characteristics. The "blueprint" for your request is essentially complete.

The final step in this preparatory phase is to translate this clarified intention into the specific building blocks – the preliminary instructions and contextual information – that will form the core of your actual prompt. This involves two small but important steps:

1. Extracting the Key Elements

Go back through your notes from the SMARTE or 5W+H exercises. Pull out the essential pieces of information and group them into logical categories. These categories typically align with the core components of a well-structured prompt (which we'll detail in Chapter 3), such as:

- **Main Objective:** What is the primary task you want the AI to perform?
- **AI Role/Persona:** How should the AI behave or what perspective should it adopt?
- **Essential Context:** What background information is crucial for the AI to understand the request?
- **Target Audience (for the output):** Who is the final response intended for?
- **Required Format:** How should the output be structured or presented?
- **Required Tone/Style:** What should the language feel and sound like?
- **Specific Constraints/Inclusions:** What must be included or excluded? Are there length limits, specific keywords, or other guardrails?

Looking back at our IT Project Manager example, the key elements extracted from the 5W+H analysis might be listed like this:

- *Objective:* Produce one-page summary of Project Z status for March.
- *AI Role:* Synthetic, factual executive assistant.
- *Context:* Project Z, Company A, focus on March updates.

- *Audience:* Steering Committee (needs synthesis, KPIs, blockers).
- *Format:* Clear bullet points, structured sections (Progress, Blockers, Next Steps).
- *Tone/Style:* Factual, professional, concise.
- *Constraints/Inclusions:* Max 1 page. Highlight 3 critical points. Focus on business impact, not deep tech details.

This step organizes your clarified thoughts into discrete, manageable pieces of information, ready to be phrased as instructions.

2. Phrasing Elements as Instructions or Context

Now, translate each of these extracted elements into clear, direct language suitable for an AI prompt. Use strong action verbs for instructions and provide contextual information plainly.

Here are some examples of how to phrase elements from different categories:

- **Objective:**
    - "Your primary objective is to..."
    - "You must generate..."
    - "The goal of this task is to analyze..."

- **AI Role/Persona:**
  - "Act as a."
  - "You are an."
  - "Adopt the perspective of a."
- **Essential Context:**
  - "Here is the necessary background context:."
  - "We are operating under the following circumstances:."
  - "Assume the following information is true:."
- **Target Audience:**
  - "The final output is intended for."
  - "Write this as if you are speaking to."
- **Required Format:**
  - "Present the information using clear bullet points."
  - "Format the output as a JSON object with the following keys: ..."
  - "Structure the response as a formal business email."
- **Required Tone/Style:**
  - "Adopt a formal and professional tone."
  - "The style should be concise and easily scannable."

- ○ "Use encouraging and empathetic language."
- **Specific Constraints/Inclusions:**
    - ○ "Limit your response to a maximum of 500 words."
    - ○ "Do not mention any specific competitor names."
    - ○ "Ensure you emphasize the cost-saving benefits."
    - ○ "Include a call to action at the end."

Applying this to our IT Project Manager example:

- "Act as a synthetic and factual executive assistant."
- "Your objective is to draft a one-page summary, using clear bullet points, covering the status of Project Z for the month of March."
- "The target audience is the Steering Committee, so focus on high-level progress, blockers requiring decisions, and key next steps."
- "The context is Project Z within Company A."
- "Structure the summary into three sections: Progress, Blockers, and Next Steps."
- "Adopt a factual, professional, and concise tone."
- "Ensure the summary does not exceed one page. Highlight the top 3 most critical issues."

You now have the clearly phrased, essential components – the "ingredients" derived from careful thought and planning – ready to be assembled into a well-structured prompt. You haven't typed into the AI interface yet, but you've already completed the most critical part of the process. You know *exactly* what you want to bake.

The next step? Learning how to combine these ingredients effectively, arranging them in the right order and structure on your "recipe card" to ensure the AI can follow your instructions perfectly. It's time to move from clarifying intent to mastering the art of prompt structure. Let's turn to Chapter 3.

3 - The Art of the Recipe Card

Structuring Your Prompt for Guaranteed Results

In Chapter 2, we undertook the crucial first step of the prompt pâtissier: **clarifying intention**. Like deciding precisely what kind of cake or pastry we intend to bake before even touching the ingredients, we learned to define our objectives using frameworks like SMARTE and 5W+H. We now possess the "building blocks" – the clearly articulated goals, context, constraints, and desired output characteristics for our AI interaction.

But having the right ingredients listed isn't enough to guarantee a culinary masterpiece. Imagine a recipe where the ingredients are simply thrown onto the page in a random jumble, with instructions mixed in haphazardly. "Add flour, preheat oven to 180°C, don't forget the vanilla, mix eggs and sugar first, bake for 30 minutes, needs chocolate chips." Following such chaotic instructions would be confusing, stressful, and likely lead to a baking disaster.

Similarly, simply listing all your carefully clarified intentions, roles, context points, and format requirements in a long, rambling paragraph for the AI is asking for trouble. While modern AI models are surprisingly adept at parsing complex inputs, presenting your request in a disorganized "kitchen sink" fashion significantly increases the risk of confusion, misinterpretation, and ultimately, disappointing results.

This chapter focuses on the next essential skill: **structuring your prompt logically and clearly**. We'll explore *why* structure is so critical for reliable AI responses, identify the essential components or "ingredients" that belong in nearly every well-crafted prompt, introduce a simple yet powerful template (C.R.O.F.T.C.) to organize these components, and demonstrate through concrete examples how structure transforms a potentially confusing request into a clear, actionable "recipe card" that guides the AI effectively towards your desired outcome. Just as a well-written recipe provides a clear path to baking success, a well-structured prompt provides a clear path to AI success.

Why Structure Isn't Optional: Avoiding the Pitfalls of the Jumbled Prompt

Have you ever written a detailed, multi-part request to an AI, only to feel like it completely ignored half of your instructions? Perhaps you asked for a summary of a specific length, in a particular tone, covering three key points, but the response was twice as long, used the wrong tone, and only addressed two of the points. It's a common frustration, and it often stems directly from a lack of clear structure in the prompt.

Remember from Chapter 1 that AI models process information sequentially, predicting the next token based on the preceding context. When a prompt is a disorganized jumble – mixing background context with core instructions, format requirements with constraints, and desired tone – it creates a noisy and potentially confusing sequence for the AI to process.

Imagine trying to follow those jumbled baking instructions. When should you preheat the oven? Did the instruction about vanilla apply to the wet or dry ingredients? How much flour was needed again? The lack of logical order makes it easy to miss steps or misinterpret the sequence.

Similarly, in a poorly structured prompt, certain crucial elements might get "lost in the noise". Instructions buried deep within a long paragraph might carry less "weight" in the AI's probabilistic calculations than those presented earlier or more clearly. A constraint mentioned offhandedly might be overlooked. The core objective might be diluted by excessive background information provided too early. The AI isn't deliberately ignoring parts of your request; its sequential processing mechanism is simply struggling to accurately prioritize and integrate instructions presented in a chaotic manner.

Let's consider a deliberately disorganized prompt for a common task: writing about remote work.

- **Messy Prompt:** *"Okay, I need a text about the rise of remote work, make it about 500 words. It should be aimed at managers who are skeptical. Could you use a fairly formal tone? Also, cover the main benefits like flexibility and wider talent pool, but definitely also address the challenges, especially communication and team cohesion issues. I need this pretty soon. Maybe start with a hook about how the pandemic changed things?"*

While all the necessary elements might *technically* be present, their jumbled presentation creates numerous risks:

- Will the AI remember the 500-word limit mentioned early on?
- Will the "formal tone" instruction, buried mid-paragraph, be consistently applied?
- Will the specific audience ("skeptical managers") truly shape the content, or will it default to a more generic overview?
- Will it give equal weight to benefits *and* challenges as requested?
- Will the suggested starting point (pandemic hook) be implemented effectively or feel tacked on?

The lack of clear separation and logical flow makes the prompt harder for the AI to parse correctly, increasing the likelihood of a response that misses one or more key requirements. It forces the AI to guess at the structure and hierarchy of importance, leading to unreliable and often incomplete results.

Just as a clear recipe card prevents baking errors, **a well-structured prompt prevents AI misinterpretations and ensures all your carefully clarified intentions are understood and addressed**. Structure isn't just about neatness; it's about clarity, reliability, and maximizing the chances of getting exactly what you need from the AI.

So, what are the essential components that form the foundation of a well-structured prompt? Let's break down the key "ingredients" that should appear on almost every prompt "recipe card".

The Essential Ingredients of a Structured Prompt

Based on our understanding of how AI works (Chapter 1) and the importance of clear intention (Chapter 2), we can identify several key categories of information that, when presented clearly and logically, significantly improve the quality and relevance of AI responses. Think of these as the core ingredients needed for almost any successful prompt recipe:

1. Context (C): Setting the Scene

- **Why it's crucial:** This is the foundation. Providing relevant background information upfront helps the AI "calibrate" its understanding and activate the most appropriate knowledge domains. It answers the implicit question: "What world are we operating in for this request?"
- **What it includes:** Necessary background on the topic, the current situation or problem, key definitions, information about the target audience

if it influences the content itself, and any other foundational details the AI needs *before* receiving the main instruction.

- **Pastry Analogy:** This is like listing the type of event the pastry is for (e.g., "a child's birthday party," "a formal wedding reception," "a casual afternoon tea"). This context immediately influences subsequent choices.

- **Example (Notary - Clause Generation):**
  - **Context:** *"We are drafting a real estate sales contract for a residential property located in Bordeaux, France. The seller is Mr. Dupont, the buyer is Ms. Durand. There is a known right-of-way servitude documented on the property title benefiting the adjacent property."* (This immediately tells the AI the legal jurisdiction, parties, property type, and a key specific issue).

Providing context first helps the AI narrow its focus from the vast ocean of its training data to the specific pond relevant to your request.

2. Role (R): Defining the AI's Persona

- **Why it's crucial:** As discussed in Chapter 1, explicitly assigning a role or persona to the AI is a powerful way to guide its tone, style, vocabulary, and perspective. It tells the AI *who* it should be while responding.

- **What it includes:** A clear statement defining the expertise, viewpoint, or character the AI should adopt (e.g., "Act as...", "You are...", "Assume the perspective of...").

- **Pastry Analogy:** This is like specifying *who* is making the pastry – a meticulous French pâtissier, a rustic Italian nonna, or a trendy molecular gastronomist. Each implies a different style and approach.

- **Example (Business Coach - Content Generation):**
    - **Role:** *"Act as an experienced and empathetic business coach who specializes in helping early-stage entrepreneurs (0-3 years) overcome imposter syndrome and build confidence."* (This sets the expertise, target audience focus, and desired tone).

The role instruction activates the specific linguistic patterns and knowledge associated with that persona in the AI's training data, leading to more tailored and authentic-sounding responses.

3. Objective (O): Stating the Core Task

- **Why it's crucial:** This is the heart of the prompt – the main instruction telling the AI what you actually want it to *do*. It should be clear, concise, and action-oriented, directly reflecting the clarified intention from Chapter 2.

- **What it includes:** The primary verb defining the task (e.g., Analyze, Draft, Summarize, Compare, Brainstorm, Generate, Explain, Translate, Code...) followed by the specifics of the task.

- **Pastry Analogy:** This is the core instruction of the recipe: "Make a three-layer sponge cake," "Prepare two dozen croissants," "Pipe meringue kisses".

- **Example (Marketing Director - Slogan Generation):**
  - **Objective:** *"Your objective is to generate 5 distinct advertising slogan ideas for our new eco-friendly running shoe (Product X). The slogans must highlight the shoe's primary benefit: its sustainable materials and low*

environmental impact." (Clear action, quantity, product, and key message angle).

A clear objective provides unambiguous direction, ensuring the AI focuses its efforts on the intended task.

4. Format (F): Specifying the Output Structure

- **Why it's crucial:** How the information is presented matters almost as much as the information itself. Specifying the desired format ensures the AI's output is immediately usable and easy to understand, saving you significant reformatting time.

- **What it includes:** Explicit instructions on the desired structure or layout of the response (e.g., "Use bullet points," "Present as a table with columns X, Y, Z," "Write in the format of a formal business letter," "Generate Python code," "Output as a JSON object," "Structure with H2 headings for each section").

- **Pastry Analogy:** This is the "plating" instruction: "Serve sliced on a platter," "Arrange in a pyramid," "Dust with powdered sugar," "Present in individual ramekins".

- **Example (HR Manager - Candidate Comparison):**
  - ○ **Format:** *"Present your analysis in a table format. The table should have three columns: 'Candidate Name', 'Key Strengths (Max 3 bullet points)', and 'Potential Areas for Development (Max 2 bullet points)'."* (Very specific structure requested).

Defining the format upfront prevents the AI from delivering a dense block of text when you needed a scannable list, or a simple paragraph when you required a structured table.

5. Tone/Style (T): Setting the Linguistic Flavor

- **Why it's crucial:** The tone (emotional quality) and style (linguistic structure) dramatically shape how the message is received and its overall effectiveness. Specifying this helps the AI generate content that aligns with your communication goals and brand voice.
- **What it includes:** Descriptors for the desired tone (e.g., formal, informal, professional, empathetic, humorous, urgent, objective, optimistic) and style

(e.g., concise, detailed, narrative, analytical, academic, journalistic, simple, technical, poetic).

- **Pastry Analogy:** This is the seasoning and flavor profile: "Make it spicy," "Ensure it's light and airy," "Aim for a rich, decadent flavor," "Keep it simple and classic".
- **Example (NGO Comms Manager - Public Appeal):**
  - **Tone/Style:** *"Adopt an inspiring and passionate tone, but also convey a sense of urgency regarding the issue. Use a simple, clear, and accessible writing style suitable for a broad general audience. Avoid jargon or overly academic language."*

Explicitly defining tone and style prevents the AI from producing overly robotic, inappropriately casual, or stylistically jarring content.

6. Constraints (C): Defining Boundaries and Guardrails

- **Why it's crucial:** Constraints act as essential guardrails, further refining the AI's output by specifying boundaries, required inclusions, or definite exclusions. They help prevent errors, ensure completeness on key points, and fine-tune the response to exact needs.

- **What it includes:** Specific limitations (e.g., word count, character limit, number of paragraphs), elements that *must* be included (e.g., specific keywords, data points, references), information or topics to *avoid* (e.g., "Do not mention competitors by name," "Avoid discussing costs"), or other specific rules.

- **Pastry Analogy:** This is like adding specific dietary notes to the recipe: "Must be gluten-free," "Ensure no nuts are used," "Decorate only with fresh berries," "The final cake must weigh exactly 1kg".

- **Example (Lawyer - Legal Memo):**
  - **Constraints:** *"Limit the entire response to a maximum of 300 words. Do not mention any specific past client names or case details. It is essential that you include a direct reference to Article L.123 of the French Commercial Code."*

Constraints provide the final layer of precision, ensuring the AI operates within defined boundaries and delivers a perfectly calibrated response.

These six components – Context, Role, Objective, Format, Tone/Style, and Constraints – form the essential building blocks of a well-structured, effective prompt. But how should they be arranged for optimal clarity?

Assembling the Recipe Card: The C.R.O.F.T.C. Template

Now that we have our key ingredients identified, we need a logical structure to assemble them – our prompt "recipe card." While various structures can work, a simple, memorable, and highly effective template uses the acronym **C.R.O.F.T.C.**, arranging the components in a sequence that generally makes sense for AI processing:

C - Context:

- Start by setting the scene. Provide the necessary background information first so the AI understands the landscape before receiving instructions.

R - Role:

- Immediately after the context, define the persona or perspective the AI should adopt. This helps frame its subsequent processing.

O - Objective:

- Clearly state the main task or goal. This is the core instruction and should follow the initial setup.

F - Format:

- Specify how you want the output structured. Defining this after the objective makes logical sense – first *what* to do, then *how* to present it.

T - Tone/Style:

- Indicate the desired linguistic flavor. Like format, this modifies the core objective and fits naturally here.

C - Constraints:

- Finally, add any specific boundaries, inclusions, or exclusions as guardrails.

Visualizing C.R.O.F.T.C.:

[--- CONTEXT ---]

Provide background info, situation, key definitions here.

[--- ROLE ---]

Define the AI's persona: "Act as..." or "You are..."

[--- OBJECTIVE ---]

State the main task clearly using action verbs.

[--- FORMAT ---]

Specify the desired output structure (list, table, email, etc.).

[--- TONE / STYLE ---]

Describe the required tone (formal, empathetic...) and style (concise, narrative...).

[--- CONSTRAINTS ---]

List any limits (word count), must-haves, or things to avoid.

This C.R.O.F.T.C. structure provides a robust and easy-to-remember framework. It ensures you cover all the essential bases in a logical flow, guiding the AI progressively from general context to specific execution details. Think of it as your go-to recipe card template.

Does Order Really Matter? The Subtle Influence of Sequence

A reasonable question arises: does the *order* in which you present these components truly matter, especially with sophisticated models like GPT-4 and beyond? Modern LLMs are indeed more robust than earlier versions at understanding complex prompts even if the structure isn't perfect. They attempt to consider the entire input context.

However, **order can still subtly influence emphasis and processing**. Remember, the AI works sequentially. Information presented earlier might slightly weigh more heavily in setting the initial direction of the probabilistic path.

The C.R.O.F.T.C. order is generally recommended because it follows a **natural logic of progressive definition**:

1. **Set the stage (Context):** Establish the universe of discourse.
2. **Define the actor (Role):** Specify the perspective within that universe.

3. **Assign the mission (Objective):** Give the main directive.

4. **Specify the presentation (Format, Tone/Style):** Refine how the mission should be executed and delivered.

5. **Add the final rules (Constraints):** Apply specific boundaries.

Starting with Context and Role helps the AI "initialize" its state correctly. Placing the core Objective centrally makes sense. Layering Format, Tone, and Constraints afterward allows for refinement without confusing the initial setup.

Could you put Constraints first or Format before Objective? Yes, and the AI would likely still *try* to follow all instructions. However, presenting information in a less logical order *might* slightly increase the risk of misinterpretation or certain elements getting less focus. Think of giving driving directions: telling someone about the tricky turn at the end *before* you tell them which road to take initially might be confusing. A logical sequence reduces cognitive load – potentially for both you and the AI.

Quick Thought Experiment: Imagine taking the components of our IT Project Manager example prompt and deliberately scrambling the order (e.g., start with

Format, then Objective, then Constraints, then Context, then Role). Read that scrambled version. Does it feel as clear or easy to follow? Probably not. While the AI might manage, providing a logical C.R.O.F.T.C. flow is simply a cleaner, more reliable practice that minimizes potential confusion.

So, while not absolutely rigid, **the C.R.O.F.T.C. sequence represents a best practice** – a logical, effective, and easy-to-implement structure for maximizing clarity and ensuring all aspects of your request are given appropriate attention by the AI. Treat it as your default recipe structure, adaptable when necessary, but a solid foundation to build upon.

From Vague Idea to Robust Prompt: C.R.O.F.T.C. in Action

Let's solidify our understanding by walking through two concrete examples, transforming common vague professional requests into well-structured, robust prompts using the C.R.O.F.T.C. framework. This is where the theory meets practice, demonstrating the tangible power of structure.

Case Study 1: Crafting an Email Marketing Campaign

The Need: Our Entrepreneur in e-commerce needs help promoting a new clothing collection. Their initial thought: *"I need an email to promote my new collection."*

The Problem: This is far too vague. What collection? Who is the email for? What should it say? What's the goal? What tone? An AI given this prompt would produce generic, unusable marketing fluff.

Applying C.R.O.F.T.C. (incorporating clarifications likely made using SMARTE/5W+H in Chapter 2):

- **C - Context:**
    - We are launching a new collection of women's apparel made from sustainable, eco-friendly materials (primarily organic cotton and recycled fibers).
    - The target audience is women aged 25-40 who are fashion-conscious but also prioritize ethical consumption and sustainability.
    - The email aims to announce the collection's arrival and drive traffic to the online store's new collection page.

- **R - Role:**
    - Act as an expert email marketing copywriter specializing in sustainable and ethical fashion brands. Your writing should be engaging and persuasive for this specific audience.
- **O - Objective:**
    - Draft a compelling email announcing the launch of the new sustainable clothing collection. The primary goal is to generate excitement and entice recipients to click through to view the collection on our website.
- **F - Format:**
    - Provide the output in a standard email format, including:
        - A catchy and intriguing Subject Line (suggest 2-3 options).
        - A concise email body (approximately 150-200 words).
        - A clear and prominent Call-to-Action (CTA) button text (e.g., "Shop the Collection Now," "Discover Sustainable Style").

- **T - Tone/Style:**
  - Adopt an enthusiastic, inspiring, and slightly exclusive tone. Make the reader feel excited about discovering something new and aligned with their values.
  - The style should be sophisticated yet accessible, reflecting a premium sustainable brand.

- **C - Constraints:**
  - Highlight the use of organic cotton as a key material feature.
  - Include a limited-time introductory offer: "-10% off the new collection for the first 48 hours."
  - Avoid overly technical jargon about fabric production; focus on the style and sustainable benefits.
  - Ensure the email is mobile-friendly in its structure (short paragraphs).

The Resulting Structured Prompt:

Code extract

[--- CONTEXT ---]

We are launching a new collection of women's apparel made from sustainable, eco-friendly materials (primarily organic cotton and recycled fibers). The target audience is women aged 25-40 who are fashion-conscious but also prioritize ethical consumption and sustainability. The email aims to announce the collection's arrival and drive traffic to the online store's new collection page.

[--- ROLE ---]

Act as an expert email marketing copywriter specializing in sustainable and ethical fashion brands. Your writing should be engaging and persuasive for this specific audience.

[--- OBJECTIVE ---]

Draft a compelling email announcing the launch of the new sustainable clothing collection. The primary goal is to generate excitement and entice recipients to click through to view the collection on our website.

[--- FORMAT ---]

Provide the output in a standard email format, including:

- A catchy and intriguing Subject Line (suggest 2-3 options).

- A concise email body (approximately 150-200 words).

- A clear and prominent Call-to-Action (CTA) button text (e.g., "Shop the Collection Now," "Discover Sustainable Style").

[--- TONE / STYLE ---]

Adopt an enthusiastic, inspiring, and slightly exclusive tone. Make the reader feel excited about discovering something new and aligned with their values. The style should be sophisticated yet accessible, reflecting a premium sustainable brand.

[--- CONSTRAINTS ---]

- Highlight the use of organic cotton as a key material feature.

- Include a limited-time introductory offer: "-10% off the new collection for the first 48 hours."

- Avoid overly technical jargon about fabric production; focus on the style and sustainable benefits.

- Ensure the email is mobile-friendly in its structure (short paragraphs).

Compare the likely output of this detailed, structured prompt to the output of the initial vague request. The structured prompt leaves far less to chance. It guides the AI precisely, increasing the probability of receiving a draft email that is relevant, targeted, appropriately toned, correctly formatted, and includes all the necessary elements – ready for minor tweaking rather than a complete rewrite. The structure transformed a fuzzy idea into actionable instructions.

Case Study 2: Synthesizing a Lengthy Meeting

The Need: Our Consultant or Project Manager has just finished a two-hour project meeting and needs a concise summary for stakeholders who couldn't attend. Their initial thought: *"Summarize this meeting transcript."* (Imagine they paste or upload the transcript).

The Problem: What kind of summary? For whom? Focusing on what? Decisions? Actions? Problems? A generic summary might be too long, miss key action items, or fail to highlight critical decisions.

Applying C.R.O.F.T.C.:

- **C - Context:**
  - Attached/Below is the raw transcript of a 2-hour virtual meeting held today regarding Project Y.
  - Key participants included Alice (Product Lead), Bob (Lead Engineer), and Charlie (Marketing Manager).
  - The meeting covered Q2 roadmap planning, resource allocation challenges, and a review of recent user feedback.
- **R - Role:**
  - Act as a highly efficient executive assistant with expertise in creating concise, actionable meeting summaries for busy executives.
- **O - Objective:**
  - Produce a concise summary of the meeting, focusing *only* on:
    - Key decisions made during the session.
    - Specific action items assigned (clearly identify the owner and deadline if mentioned in the transcript).

- Any major unresolved issues or points requiring further discussion/escalation.

- **F - Format:**
  - Structure the summary using clear bullet points.
  - Organize the bullet points under three distinct headings: "Key Decisions," "Action Items," and "Pending Issues / Points for Escalation."
  - The entire summary must fit on a single page (approximately 300-400 words maximum).

- **T - Tone/Style:**
  - Adopt a purely factual, neutral, and professional tone.
  - The style must be extremely concise and objective. Avoid interpretations or opinions.

- **C - Constraints:**
  - Extract *only* information directly related to decisions, actions, and unresolved issues. Ignore off-topic discussions, general brainstorming, or lengthy debates unless they directly resulted in one of these outcomes.

- ○ For each action item, clearly state the item, the assigned owner's name (Alice, Bob, or Charlie), and the deadline, if specified in the transcript. **Bold** the owner's name.
- ○ If an owner or deadline for an action is unclear from the transcript, note that explicitly (e.g., "Action: - Owner: Unclear, Deadline: Not specified").

The Resulting Structured Prompt:

Code extract

[--- CONTEXT ---]

Attached/Below is the raw transcript of a 2-hour virtual meeting held today regarding Project Y. Key participants included Alice (Product Lead), Bob (Lead Engineer), and Charlie (Marketing Manager). The meeting covered Q2 roadmap planning, resource allocation challenges, and a review of recent user feedback.

[--- ROLE ---]

Act as a highly efficient executive assistant with expertise in creating concise, actionable meeting summaries for busy executives.

[--- OBJECTIVE ---]

Produce a concise summary of the meeting, focusing *only* on:

- Key decisions made during the session.

- Specific action items assigned (clearly identify the owner and deadline if mentioned in the transcript).

- Any major unresolved issues or points requiring further discussion/escalation.

[--- FORMAT ---]

- Structure the summary using clear bullet points.

- Organize the bullet points under three distinct headings: "Key Decisions," "Action Items," and "Pending Issues / Points for Escalation."

- The entire summary must fit on a single page (approximately 300-400 words maximum).

[--- TONE / STYLE ---]

- Adopt a purely factual, neutral, and professional tone.

- The style must be extremely concise and objective. Avoid interpretations or opinions.

[--- CONSTRAINTS ---]

- Extract *only* information directly related to decisions, actions, and unresolved issues. Ignore off-topic discussions, general brainstorming, or lengthy debates unless they directly resulted in one of these outcomes.

- For each action item, clearly state the item, the assigned owner's name (Alice, Bob, or Charlie), and the deadline, if specified in the transcript. **Bold** the owner's name.

- If an owner or deadline for an action is unclear from the transcript, note that explicitly (e.g., "Action: - Owner: Unclear, Deadline: Not specified").

Again, the structured C.R.O.F.T.C. prompt provides vastly superior guidance compared to the initial vague request. It tells the AI exactly what information to extract, how to format it, the perspective to adopt, and the rules to follow. This dramatically increases the likelihood of receiving a summary that is immediately useful, accurate, and saves the consultant or project manager significant time and effort. The structure provides the clarity needed for a high-quality, targeted output.

These examples demonstrate that the C.R.O.F.T.C. framework isn't just a theoretical concept; it's a practical tool applicable across a wide range of professional tasks. It provides a reliable method for translating your clarified intentions (Chapter 2) into clear, unambiguous instructions that leverage your understanding of the AI (Chapter 1).

You now have the "recipe card" structure. You know the essential ingredients and a logical way to arrange them. But just as knowing the structure of a recipe isn't enough – the *precision* of the measurements and the *nuance* of the technique are what elevate pastry from good to great – the same applies to prompts. The next chapter delves into this crucial aspect: the "chef's touch," the art of precision in your language, formatting requests, and constraints. It's time to learn why every word matters.

4 - The Precision of the Grammage

Why Every Word Counts in Your Prompt

We've laid a strong foundation. We understand our AI "oven" – its predictive nature and limitations (Chapter 1). We've mastered the crucial art of clarifying our intention – knowing exactly *what* we want to bake before we begin (Chapter 2). And we've learned how to structure our request logically using the C.R.O.F.T.C. template – our reliable "recipe card" (Chapter 3).

Now, we arrive at the stage where true mastery begins to emerge. It's the difference between a home cook following a recipe adequately and a master chef executing it with finesse. It's the *precision*, the *nuance*, the attention to the seemingly small details that collectively elevate the final creation from good to extraordinary.

In pastry, this means understanding the precise "grammage" – knowing that 10 grams too much flour can make a cake dense, that the exact temperature of melted butter matters, that the *type* of vanilla extract impacts the final flavor profile. It's also about the "tour de main" – the skillful techniques in folding, mixing, piping, and plating.

In prompt engineering, this translates to **precision in language and instruction**. It means recognizing that *every word* in your prompt carries weight. The specific verbs and adjectives you choose, the way you define the desired tone and style, the clarity of your formatting requests, the strategic use of constraints, and even the power of providing concrete examples – these are the details that allow you to fine-tune the AI's output with remarkable control.

This chapter delves into that precision. We'll explore how seemingly minor choices in wording can dramatically shift the AI's response, how to consciously shape the "how" (the style, tone, and perspective) of the output, the importance of specifying format and length meticulously, the surprising power of telling the AI what *not* to do, and an advanced technique for literally *showing* the AI what you expect. Get ready to refine your technique – it's time to master the prompt pâtissier's delicate touch.

From Generic to Specific: The Surprising Power of Verbs and Adjectives

Think about the action words you use in everyday communication. Do "summarize," "synthesize," "analyze," and "critique" all mean the same thing to you? Perhaps roughly, but each carries a distinct nuance. "Summarize" implies brevity and hitting the main points. "Synthesize" suggests combining information from multiple sources into a coherent whole. "Analyze" involves breaking something down into its constituent parts. "Critique" requires evaluation and judgment.

While humans might sometimes use these terms loosely, for an AI operating on statistical patterns, these distinctions can be significant. **Choosing your verbs and adjectives with intention is perhaps the most fundamental aspect of prompt precision**. It's the difference between asking vaguely for "some sugar" versus specifying "50 grams of caster sugar."

Action Verbs: Directing the Core Task

The primary verb in your Objective statement sets the fundamental direction for the AI. Consider the difference between:

- **"Describe the process..."** (Focus on outlining steps, observation) vs. **"Analyze the process..."** (Focus on breaking down components, identifying relationships, potentially evaluating effectiveness).
- **"List the features..."** (Simple enumeration) vs. **"Create a compelling narrative around the features..."** (Requires storytelling, benefit-oriented language).
- **"Compare options A and B..."** (Highlight similarities and differences) vs. **"Evaluate options A and B..."** (Requires judgment, potentially recommending one over the other based on criteria).

Using a generic verb like "Tell me about..." or "Write about..." gives the AI maximum leeway, often resulting in a response that doesn't quite hit the mark. Choosing a *precise* action verb immediately focuses the AI's efforts on the specific cognitive task you intend for it to perform.

Adjectives and Adverbs: Refining the Nuance

Beyond the core verb, descriptive words add crucial layers of specificity. They act like the subtle adjustments in seasoning or temperature that refine a dish. Consider:

- "Provide an **objective** analysis..." vs. "Provide a **critical** analysis..."
- "Generate a **concise** summary..." vs. "Generate a **detailed** summary..."
- "Write in a **formal** tone..." vs. "Write in an **empathetic** tone..."
- "Respond **briefly**..." vs. "Respond **comprehensively**..."

These modifiers guide the AI's approach to fulfilling the objective. They signal the desired depth, perspective, style, or emotional quality of the response. Ignoring them or using vague descriptors leaves these crucial aspects open to the AI's interpretation (i.e., statistical default), which may not align with your needs. This level of detail is the "precision grammage" of prompting.

Putting it Together: The Impact of Precision

Let's illustrate the combined effect with a comparison:

- **Prompt A (Less Precise):** *"Tell me about the impact of AI on jobs."*
  - *Expected Outcome:* Likely a very general overview, possibly touching on automation, job creation, and skills gaps, but lacking depth, specific context, or a

clear analytical stance. It might resemble a basic encyclopedia entry.

- **Prompt B (More Precise):** *"Acting as a labor market economist,* **critically analyze** *the* **potential impacts** *(both* **positive** *and* **negative***) of generative AI technologies on* **white-collar employment** *within the* **French tertiary sector** *over the* **next 5 years***. Focus on* **quantifiable shifts** *where possible and consider implications for skills demand. Present your analysis in a* **structured essay format** *(approx. 800 words) with* **clear headings** *for positive and negative impacts."*

  - *Expected Outcome:* A much more focused, nuanced, and analytical response. The specific role ("economist"), action verb ("critically analyze"), qualifiers ("potential," "positive and negative"), context ("white-collar," "French tertiary sector," "next 5 years"), required elements ("quantifiable shifts," "skills demand"), and format ("structured essay," "800 words," "headings") combine to guide the AI towards a high-value, specific output tailored to a professional need.

The difference is stark. The precision embedded in Prompt B acts like a detailed recipe, guiding the AI through a complex task with clarity, while Prompt A is like vaguely asking for "something about jobs and AI." **Choosing your words with care isn't pedantry; it's the fundamental mechanism for ensuring the AI's output aligns precisely with your strategic intention.**

But precision goes beyond just the core task definition. It also extends to shaping the overall feel and presentation of the response – the "how" it communicates, not just the "what".

Defining the "How": Shaping Style, Tone, and Perspective

A perfectly executed pastry isn't just technically flawless; it also has character. It might be playful, elegant, rustic, or avant-garde. Similarly, an effective AI response often needs more than just accurate information; it needs the right **tone**, **style**, and sometimes even a specific **perspective** to truly resonate and achieve its purpose. Consciously defining these "how" elements in your prompt is crucial for moving beyond generic output to truly impactful communication.

Tone: Setting the Emotional Temperature

Tone refers to the overall feeling, attitude, or emotional quality conveyed by the language. Do you want the AI's response to sound formal and authoritative, warm and friendly, urgent and alarming, calm and reassuring, humorous and witty, or perhaps strictly neutral and objective?

The tone can dramatically alter how the information is received and interpreted. Consider asking for advice on a difficult conversation:

- A prompt asking for "advice" might yield generic, impersonal steps.
- A prompt asking the AI to "Act as an empathetic and supportive mentor and provide advice..." will likely yield a response using softer language, acknowledging feelings, and offering encouragement – potentially far more helpful in that context.

How to specify tone:

- Use explicit instructions: "Adopt a tone." (e.g., formal, informal, professional, casual, empathetic, objective, optimistic, concerned, urgent, playful, serious).

- Use descriptive language: "Write in a warm and encouraging manner," "Maintain a strictly neutral and factual voice," "Use language that conveys expertise and confidence".
- Combine with Role: The assigned Role often implies a tone (e.g., "Act as a stern drill sergeant" vs. "Act as a gentle kindergarten teacher").

Exercise: Ask your AI to describe a simple object, like a cup of coffee, using three different tones:

1. Tone: Enthusiastic and promotional (like a coffee shop ad).
2. Tone: Technical and analytical (like a chemist describing its composition).
3. Tone: Poetic and evocative (like a novelist describing a character's morning ritual). Observe how the word choices, sentence structures, and overall feeling change dramatically based *only* on the requested tone.

Mastering tone allows you to shape the reader's experience and ensure the AI's communication lands with the intended emotional impact.

Style: Crafting the Linguistic Structure

While tone deals with the feeling, **style** relates more to the structure, vocabulary, and density of the language itself. It answers questions like:

- How complex should the sentences be?
- Should the vocabulary be simple or sophisticated? Technical or accessible?
- Should the writing be concise or elaborate? Narrative or analytical? Bullet points or prose?

Different styles suit different purposes and audiences. A legal brief requires a vastly different style than a blog post, which differs again from ad copy or a scientific paper.

How to specify style:

- Use explicit style labels: "Use a journalistic style," "Write in an academic style," "Adopt a conversational blog post style," "Format as a technical manual section".
- Provide descriptive instructions: "Use short, simple sentences," "Employ vivid, descriptive language," "Maintain a highly structured, logical flow," "Focus on clear, actionable bullet points".
- Reference examples (implicitly or explicitly): "Write in the style of" (use with caution, as AI's

interpretation varies) or provide a short sample paragraph demonstrating the desired style within the prompt itself (a form of few-shot prompting, see Argument 4.5).

Exercise: Ask the AI to explain a concept you know reasonably well (e.g., the basic idea of prompt engineering itself) using two distinct styles:

1. Style: "Science popularization for a general audience" (like a magazine article).
2. Style: "Technical documentation for software engineers" (like a user manual). Notice the differences in vocabulary, sentence length, use of examples, and overall structure.

Defining the style ensures the AI's output is not only accurate but also appropriate for its intended context and readership. It prevents the jarring experience of receiving a highly technical explanation when you needed a simple overview, or a casual blog post when you required a formal report.

Perspective: Adopting a Specific Point of View

Beyond tone and style, you can ask the AI to adopt a specific **perspective** or viewpoint when analyzing a situation or generating content. This is a powerful technique for uncovering hidden assumptions, exploring different facets of an issue, and stimulating creative thinking.

Instead of just asking for an analysis, you might ask the AI to perform the analysis *from the viewpoint of*:

- A potential investor focusing on ROI and risk.
- An end-user frustrated with product usability.
- A competitor looking for strategic weaknesses.
- An environmental activist concerned about sustainability.
- A specific historical figure considering a modern problem.

Forcing the AI to adopt a specific lens often surfaces insights and arguments that might be missed in a neutral analysis. It pushes the AI beyond generic statements and encourages it to consider the implications from a particular angle. This is especially valuable in strategic planning, risk assessment, or creative brainstorming, where considering diverse viewpoints is crucial.

Exercise: Think of a recent business decision or proposal in your field (e.g., launching a new feature, changing a pricing model, adopting a new technology). Ask the AI to analyze the pros and cons of this decision successively from three different perspectives:

1. The perspective of the Chief Marketing Officer (focused on customer acquisition and brand).
2. The perspective of the Chief Financial Officer (focused on cost, revenue, and profitability).
3. The perspective of a long-term, loyal customer (focused on value and user experience). Compare the arguments and concerns raised from each perspective. Notice how adopting a specific viewpoint changes the focus and highlights different facets of the decision.

Skillfully using perspective prompts allows you to leverage the AI as a multi-faceted sparring partner, exploring problems from angles you might not have considered otherwise, enriching your analysis and decision-making.

Mastering the "how" – tone, style, and perspective – adds a crucial layer of finesse to your prompting. But precision also extends to the very tangible *shape* of the output you receive.

Specifying the Tangible Output: Format and Length

Imagine ordering a custom piece of furniture. You wouldn't just describe the style; you'd provide exact dimensions, specify the type of wood, the finish, the number of drawers. Similarly, when requesting information or content from an AI, being precise about the desired **format** and **length** is essential for ensuring the output is not only conceptually correct but also practically usable.

Beyond Plain Text: The Power of Formatting

Left to its own devices, an AI will typically default to generating paragraphs of text. But often, that's not the most effective or efficient way to present information. Explicitly requesting a specific format can save you enormous amounts of time in re-organizing or re-presenting the AI's output.

Consider the wide range of formats you can request:

- **Lists:**
    - **Bullet points:** Ideal for summaries, key takeaways, feature lists, brainstorming output. (e.g., "List the pros and cons as bullet points.")
    - **Numbered lists:** Best for sequential steps, rankings, or ordered instructions. (e.g., "Provide step-by-step instructions as a numbered list.")

- **Tables:**
  - Excellent for comparing items across specific criteria, organizing data, presenting structured information concisely. You *must* specify the columns and ideally the rows or items to compare. (e.g., "Create a table comparing features A, B, and C with columns for 'Feature', 'Benefit', and 'Implementation Effort'.")
- **Code:**
  - Request code snippets in specific programming languages (Python, JavaScript, HTML, CSS, SQL, etc.). Be precise about the required functionality, libraries, or context. (e.g., "Write a Python function that takes a list of numbers and returns the average.")
- **Structured Data Formats:**
  - **JSON:** Ideal for passing data to other applications or for structured machine processing. Specify the desired key-value structure. (e.g., "Output the extracted information as a JSON object with keys 'name', 'email', and 'company'.")
  - **CSV:** Useful for tabular data that needs to be imported into spreadsheets. Specify the

delimiter if needed. (e.g., "Generate sample customer data in CSV format with columns: ID, Name, City.")

- **Specific Document Types:**
  - Ask the AI to structure the response like a particular document. (e.g., "Draft this as a formal business email," "Write this in the format of a press release," "Structure this like a blog post with an introduction, H2 headings for sections, and a conclusion," "Generate a meeting agenda.")

- **Dialogue/Script:**
  - Useful for generating conversational examples, role-playing scenarios, or video scripts. (e.g., "Write a short dialogue between a customer and a support agent resolving issue X.")

How to specify format:

- Be explicit and unambiguous: "Present the results **as a table** with..." "Use **bullet points** for the summary." "Format the output **as JSON**."
- Provide details: If requesting a table, name the columns. If JSON, suggest the keys. If a list, specify numbered or bulleted.

Requesting the right format upfront transforms the AI from a text generator into a multi-purpose content structuring tool, delivering information in a way that's immediately ready for your specific use case.

Taming the Verbosity: Mastering Length Constraints

Another common frustration is receiving AI responses that are wildly too long or frustratingly too short for your needs. While AIs don't have perfect control over exact word counts, providing clear guidance on the desired **length** is crucial for getting appropriately scoped output.

How to specify length:

- **Word Count:** "Limit the response to approximately words." (e.g., 100 words, 500 words). Be aware this is often an approximation.
- **Sentence/Paragraph Count:** "Summarize this in no more than 3 sentences." "Provide 5 distinct paragraphs."
- **Page Limits:** "Ensure the entire summary fits on a single page."
- **Qualitative Descriptors:** Use terms that imply length and detail level: "Provide a **brief** overview," "Write a **concise** summary," "Generate a **detailed** analysis," "Give a **comprehensive** explanation".

These often work well in conjunction with numeric limits.

Exercise: Take a short article or a section from a previous AI response.

1. Ask the AI: *"Summarize the provided text in approximately 50 words."*
2. Ask the AI (in a new prompt): *"Summarize the provided text in approximately 200 words, ensuring you cover the main points in more detail."* Compare the outputs. Notice how the level of detail and the information included changes based *only* on the length constraint.

Guiding the length is essential for tailoring the AI's output to your specific need – whether you require a quick, scannable executive summary or a deep, thorough exploration of a topic. Like adjusting the size of your pastry mould, specifying length ensures the final product fits the intended purpose.

But what about refining the content itself? Sometimes, the most effective way to guide the AI is not by telling it what to include, but by telling it what to *leave out*.

The Sculptor's Chisel: Using Negative Constraints to Refine

Think of a sculptor working with a block of marble. They don't just add clay; a large part of their process involves carefully chipping away the unwanted material to reveal the desired form within. Similarly, effective prompting sometimes involves telling the AI precisely what *not* to do or include – using **negative constraints**.

While positive instructions ("Do this," "Include that") are essential, negative constraints ("Don't do that," "Avoid this") act as powerful sculpting tools, helping you carve away irrelevant, undesirable, or potentially problematic elements from the AI's response. They add another layer of precision by defining clear boundaries.

Common Uses of Negative Constraints:

- **Avoiding Topics/Information:** "Do not discuss pricing." "Avoid mentioning our past failures on Project X." "Don't include any information from before the year 2020."
- **Excluding Jargon/Complexity:** "Do not use technical jargon; explain in simple terms." "Avoid overly academic language."

- **Preventing Stereotypes/Clichés:** "Avoid clichés commonly associated with." "Do not use gendered language or assumptions."
- **Filtering Solutions/Ideas:** "Suggest solutions that do *not* require a significant budget increase." "Brainstorm ideas, but avoid anything related to social media."
- **Controlling Tone/Style Negatively:** "Do not use humor." "Avoid an overly salesy tone."

How to phrase negative constraints:

- Use clear negative imperatives: "Do not...", "Avoid...", "Exclude...", "Never mention..."
- Be specific about what to exclude. "Avoid negativity" is less effective than "Avoid mentioning specific risks associated with..."

Example Exercise: Let's say you're using AI to brainstorm potential names for a new artisanal bakery.

1. *Initial Prompt:* "Brainstorm 10 potential names for a new artisanal bakery." (Likely to include common bakery words like "Bread," "Oven," "Crust," etc.)
2. *Refined Prompt with Negative Constraint:* "Brainstorm 10 potential names for a new artisanal bakery. **Do not use common bakery-related**

words like 'Bread', 'Oven', 'Crust', 'Loaf', 'Pastry', or 'Dough'. Focus on names evoking warmth, community, or natural ingredients." Compare the likely outputs. The second prompt, by explicitly excluding the obvious, forces the AI to be more creative and generate more unique or evocative names (e.g., "The Hearthstone," "Grain & Gather," "Willow Bakehouse").

Negative constraints are like the final, precise chisels used by the sculptor. They allow you to remove imperfections, sharpen edges, and ensure the final output perfectly matches your vision by clearly defining what *doesn't* belong.

We've now covered precision in core language, tone, style, perspective, format, length, and even exclusions. There's one more powerful technique in the prompt pâtissier's repertoire, particularly useful for complex or nuanced tasks: learning by example.

Show, Don't Just Tell: The Power of Examples (Few-Shot Prompting)

Imagine trying to teach someone a complex new skill – perhaps a specific writing style, a particular method of analysis, or how to classify customer feedback. You could spend a long time *explaining* the rules and principles in abstract terms. Or, you could simply *show* them a few clear examples of the desired outcome. Often, learning by example is far more efficient and effective.

The same principle applies to guiding AI. Instead of relying solely on descriptive instructions, you can provide the AI with concrete examples of the input-output pattern you want it to follow. This technique is known as **few-shot prompting**.

How it Works:

The core idea is simple: within your main prompt, you include one or more complete demonstrations of the task before posing your actual request. Each example typically consists of:

- An input (similar to the one you'll eventually provide).
- The corresponding desired output.

By seeing these examples, the AI learns the pattern, format, style, or type of reasoning you expect. It essentially infers the underlying "rule" from the demonstrations you provide. This is incredibly powerful for tasks where:

- The desired output format is complex or unusual.

- The required tone or style is very specific and hard to describe.
- The task involves a type of reasoning or transformation that's easier to show than explain.
- You want to ensure consistency in how the AI handles similar inputs.

Example: Sentiment Classification

Let's say you want the AI to classify customer feedback comments as Positive, Negative, or Neutral. You could try to explain the rules, but providing examples is often clearer:

Code extract

Classify the sentiment of the following customer feedback comments.

Text: "I absolutely love this new feature! It saves me so much time."

Sentiment: Positive

Text: "The checkout process was confusing and I almost gave up."

Sentiment: Negative

Text: "The delivery arrived on the scheduled date."

Sentiment: Neutral

Text: "Wow, the customer support team responded incredibly quickly and solved my issue immediately. Amazing service!"

Sentiment: ???

By providing three clear examples, you've shown the AI the desired input-output format and the kind of classification expected. When it encounters the final "Text:" line, it's highly likely to correctly infer the pattern and output "Positive".

Other Use Cases for Few-Shot Prompting:

- **Specific Formatting:** Show examples of how you want data extracted and formatted.
- **Code Generation:** Provide an example of input data and the desired output code structure.
- **Summarization Style:** Give an example of a long text and the kind of concise, bulleted summary you prefer.

- **Creative Writing Style:** Include a short paragraph written in the exact stylistic voice you want the AI to emulate.
- **Complex Instructions:** Break down a task by showing how to handle a simpler version first.

Important Considerations:

- **Quality of Examples:** Your examples must be accurate and perfectly represent the desired output. Garbage examples lead to garbage results.
- **Number of Examples:** "Few-shot" typically means 1 to 5 examples. Too many can make the prompt overly long and confusing. Often, just one or two well-chosen examples are sufficient.
- **Clarity:** Ensure the structure of your examples is clear, making it easy for the AI to distinguish between the input part and the output part of each demonstration.

Few-shot prompting is admittedly a more advanced technique, requiring careful construction of the examples. However, for tasks demanding high precision, specific formatting, or nuanced styles, it is often the most effective way to communicate your exact requirements to the AI, moving beyond description to direct demonstration.

With this chapter, you've added the crucial layer of precision to your prompting toolkit. You understand why every word matters, how to shape the tone and style, the importance of format and length, the power of negative constraints, and the effectiveness of learning by example. You're no longer just assembling the basic ingredients; you're mastering the fine techniques, the "precision grammage," that distinguish the proficient cook from the true prompt pâtissier.

You now possess the knowledge to clarify your intent (Chapter 2), structure your request logically (Chapter 3), and refine the details with precision (Chapter 4). But what happens when, despite all this careful preparation, the first "bake" doesn't come out perfectly? What if the AI's response, even to a well-crafted prompt, still isn't quite right?

This is where the final core skill of the strategic prompter comes into play: the art of tasting, adjusting, and refining. It's time to embrace the iterative nature of the process and learn how to effectively dialogue with the AI to co-create the perfect result. Let's move on to Chapter 5: the essential art of iteration.

5 - Taste, Adjust, Repeat

The Art of Iteration and Dialogue with AI

We've meticulously followed the prompt pâtissier's process so far. We've peered into the "oven" to understand the AI's predictive mechanics (Chapter 1). We've learned the crucial step of deciding exactly *what* we want to bake by clarifying our intention (Chapter 2). We've drafted a clear and logical "recipe card" using the C.R.O.F.T.C. structure (Chapter 3). And we've honed our technique, focusing on the "precision grammage" of language, format, tone, and constraints (Chapter 4).

You've crafted what feels like a perfect prompt – clear, structured, precise. You hit Enter, anticipating an equally perfect result. And sometimes, gratifyingly, that's exactly what happens. The AI delivers precisely what you envisioned.

But often, especially with complex or nuanced requests, the first output isn't quite right. Maybe it's 80% there, but misses a key point. Perhaps the tone is slightly off. Maybe it misinterpreted one constraint or included a minor factual error. It's like pulling a cake out of the oven – it looks good, smells right, but perhaps it's slightly underbaked in the center, or the flavor isn't perfectly balanced.

What happens next is critically important. The novice prompter might feel frustrated, concluding "AI just isn't good enough for this task," and abandon the effort. The strategic prompter, however, recognizes this moment not as failure, but as a natural and necessary part of the process. They understand that, just like in cooking, **tasting, adjusting, and refining is where true mastery lies**.

This chapter dives into the essential art of **iteration and dialogue**. We'll dismantle the persistent myth of the "perfect first prompt," establishing iteration as the expected norm. You'll learn how to systematically analyze the AI's response to pinpoint its shortcomings. We'll explore practical techniques for refining your prompts – both by modifying the initial instruction and by engaging in constructive follow-up dialogue with the AI. And finally, we'll discuss the crucial "Growth Mindset" required to view this iterative process not as a chore, but as the most effective path to truly exceptional results.

Demolishing the Myth: Why Iteration Isn't Failure, It's Method

In our quest for efficiency, it's tempting to believe that a sufficiently well-crafted prompt should yield a perfect result on the very first try. We invest time clarifying intent, structuring the request, choosing precise words – surely, that should be enough? To expect anything less feels like admitting inadequacy, either in our prompting skills or in the AI's capabilities.

This expectation, however, is largely a myth. It's like believing a Michelin-starred chef creates a groundbreaking new dish flawlessly on their first attempt. The reality of any creative or complex endeavor – whether it's cooking, writing, coding, designing, or strategic planning – involves trial, error, and refinement.

Think about our pastry chef:

- They taste the batter: Is it sweet enough? Does it need more vanilla?
- They check the bake: Is the crust golden? Is the center set? Maybe it needs five more minutes?
- They refine the garnish: Does a sprinkle of sea salt enhance the caramel? Is the chocolate drizzle too thick?

This constant cycle of **create -> evaluate -> adjust** is not a sign of incompetence; it's the *hallmark* of expertise. It's how good becomes great, and great becomes exceptional.

The same applies absolutely to prompt engineering. Given the complexity of language, the nuances of context, and the probabilistic nature of AI, expecting a perfect output from a single prompt, especially for non-trivial tasks, is often unrealistic.

Iteration – the process of refining your prompt based on the AI's response – is not a workaround for poor initial prompting. It *is* the method.. It's an integral part of the dialogue, the expected path to achieving high-quality, tailored results.

As expert N. Ponomarenko notes, "It's not about a single perfect prompt; it's about experimenting with various prompts" to solve your problem. The goal isn't necessarily a flawless first shot, but rather an efficient process of convergence towards the desired outcome through intelligent refinement.

Consider this brief, anonymized story: A consultant was using AI to generate different strategic scenarios based on a complex set of market variables. They spent considerable time crafting a detailed C.R.O.F.T.C. prompt, including context, role, objective, format, and constraints. The first response was decent – it generated plausible scenarios – but they lacked the creative edge the consultant sought. Instead of giving up, they iterated. First, they added a constraint: "Avoid overly conventional or predictable scenarios." The next output was more interesting. Then, they added a perspective shift: "Regenerate the most promising scenario from the viewpoint of a disruptive startup aiming to capture market share." *That* iteration yielded the truly insightful, "wow" result they needed. Three iterations, building on a solid initial prompt, were required to reach excellence. This wasn't failure; it was skillful refinement.

So, the first crucial step is a **mindset shift**. Release the pressure of needing to craft the "perfect" prompt immediately. Instead, aim to create a *strong initial prompt* based on the principles from Chapters 2, 3, and 4, and fully expect – even plan – to refine it based on the AI's output. Embrace iteration as the standard operating procedure for sophisticated AI interaction.

But effective iteration requires more than just willingness; it requires skillful analysis. How do you "taste" the AI's response to know *what* needs adjusting?

Analyzing the Output: How to "Taste" the AI's Response

The AI delivers its first response. Your cursor blinks. Now what? Resist the urge to either immediately accept it flaws-and-all or instantly dismiss it as useless. The next step is crucial: **perform a structured analysis of the output, comparing it critically against your original, clarified intention**. Just as a chef tastes critically, evaluating flavor, texture, and temperature against their vision for the dish, you need to evaluate the AI's response against the specific requirements you defined.

This analysis shouldn't be haphazard. Use the clarity you gained in Chapter 2 (your SMARTE objective or 5W+H points) and the structure you defined in Chapter 3 (your C.R.O.F.T.C. components) as your evaluation framework. Ask yourself a series of targeted questions:

1. Objective Alignment:

* Did the response directly address the core Objective stated in my prompt? Did it perform the main task requested?

* Is the scope of the response appropriate? Did it cover everything I asked for, or did it miss key aspects? Did it include irrelevant information?

2. Content & Accuracy:

* Is the information provided factually accurate? (Crucially important! Requires external verification, especially for critical information – recall Chapter 1.4 on hallucinations).

* Is the analysis sound? Is the reasoning logical (as far as AI reasoning goes)?

* Are the examples relevant? Are the arguments well-supported (if applicable)?

3. Format & Structure:

* Did the AI adhere to the requested Format? (e.g., bullet points, table, JSON, email structure?).

* Is the information organized logically and easy to follow? Does it respect requested headings or sections?

4. Tone & Style:

* Does the response match the specified Tone? (e.g., formal, empathetic, humorous?).

* Does it follow the requested Style? (e.g., concise, detailed, academic, conversational?).

* Does it sound appropriate for the intended Audience and the assigned Role?

5. Constraints & Context:

* Did the response respect all specified Constraints? (e.g., word count, exclusions, mandatory inclusions?).

* Does the response seem appropriately grounded in the provided Context?

6. Overall Quality & Usefulness:

* What parts of the response are particularly good or useful?

* What specific parts fall short or need improvement?

* How much editing or rework would be required to make this output meet my original goal?

To make this systematic, consider creating a simple **Response Analysis Checklist** based on your C.R.O.F.T.C. structure and your specific SMARTE/5W+H objectives for that prompt.

Checklist Item	Evaluation (Met / Partially Met / Not Met)	Notes / Specific Issues
Objective: Met?		e.g., "Addressed core task but missed secondary analysis."
Context: Reflected?		e.g., "Seems grounded in the provided background."
Role: Embodied?		e.g., "Started well but drifted from the expert persona."
Format: Correct?		e.g., "Used paragraphs instead of requested bullet points."

Tone: Appropriate?		e.g., "Tone was too informal for the intended audience."
Style: Correct?		e.g., "Too verbose, needed to be more concise."
Constraints: Respected?		e.g., "Exceeded word count," "Included forbidden topic X."
Accuracy: Verified?		e.g., "Fact-checked claim Y - it's incorrect."
Completeness: Covered?		e.g., "Only provided 2 examples when 5 were requested."

Overall Usefulness:		e.g., "Good starting point but needs significant rework on section 3."

Exercise: Find a recent response you received from an AI that wasn't quite perfect. Using the checklist above (or one you adapt), perform a structured analysis. Compare the response rigorously against what you *intended* to get. Identify the *specific* areas where it fell short. This practice sharpens your analytical eye.

This structured analysis is the diagnostic phase. Instead of just feeling vaguely dissatisfied, you now have a precise understanding of *what* is wrong and *why*. This diagnosis is the essential prerequisite for the next step: applying the right treatment to correct the course. How do we actually refine the prompt or guide the AI towards a better outcome?

Course Correction: Techniques for Refining Your Prompts

Once you've diagnosed the shortcomings of the AI's response by comparing it to your clarified intention, you have two primary ways to iterate and steer towards a better outcome:

1. **Reformulate the Initial Prompt:** Modify your original C.R.O.F.T.C. prompt to be clearer, more precise, or better structured, then run it again.
2. **Engage in Dialogue:** Use follow-up prompts in the same conversation thread to ask the AI to modify, correct, or elaborate on its *previous* response.

Often, the best approach involves a combination of both. Let's explore techniques for each.

Technique 1: Refining the Original Recipe (Prompt Reformulation)

Sometimes, the analysis reveals a fundamental flaw or omission in your *initial* prompt. Maybe it was more ambiguous than you realized, lacked critical context, or the structure wasn't quite right. In these cases, simply asking the AI to "try again" is unlikely to help. You need to revise the recipe itself. Here are common reformulation strategies:

a) Injecting More Precision (Sharpening the Details):

-   **Problem:** The response is too vague, generic, or superficial.

- **Solution:** Go back to your C.R.O.F.T.C. prompt and add more detail, especially in the Objective, Format, Tone/Style, and Constraints sections.
  - Use more specific verbs and adjectives (Chapter 4.1).
  - Define the tone or style with greater nuance (Chapter 4.2).
  - Add stricter constraints (e.g., word count, specific elements to include) (Chapter 4.4).
  - Consider adding a clear example (few-shot prompting) if appropriate (Chapter 4.5).
- **Example:**
  - *Initial Prompt Snippet (Objective):* "Generate marketing ideas." -> *Vague Response.*
  - *Revised Prompt Snippet (Objective):* "Generate 5 **low-cost** marketing ideas specifically for attracting **new freelance clients** to my **web design business**, focusing on **online strategies** suitable for a **limited budget** (under $100/month)." -> *Much More Targeted Response.*

Often, simply adding layers of specificity is the most direct way to elevate a generic response.

b) Clarifying Ambiguity (Untangling the Instructions):

- **Problem:** The AI seems to have misunderstood a key part of your request, perhaps interpreting a word or phrase differently than you intended.

- **Solution:** Review your original prompt for any terms, phrases, or instructions that could have multiple meanings. Rephrase them to be unambiguous. If an instruction was very complex, consider breaking it down into two or more simpler, sequential instructions within the prompt. (Recall Chapter 2's focus on clarity).

- **Example:**
  - *Ambiguous Prompt Snippet:* "Compare the impact of Strategy A and Strategy B on user engagement and revenue." (Does "and" mean consider both jointly, or analyze each separately?)
  - *Clarified Prompt Snippet:* "First, analyze the impact of Strategy A on user engagement. Second, analyze its impact on revenue. Third, do the same for Strategy B (analyze engagement, then revenue). Finally, provide a summary table comparing the impacts of A vs. B across both metrics."

Actively hunting down and eliminating ambiguity in your prompt is crucial for preventing AI misinterpretations.

c) Adjusting Structure or Role (Reframing the Request):

- **Problem:** The response is disorganized, illogical, or adopts the wrong perspective despite your instructions.
- **Solution:** Experiment with the *structure* of your C.R.O.F.T.C. prompt. While the default order is good, perhaps for a very complex task, putting a key Constraint earlier might help. More commonly, consider if the assigned **Role** was specific enough or perhaps the *wrong* role for the task. Redefining the AI's persona can significantly alter its approach.
- **Example:**
  - *Initial Prompt Snippet:* "Act as a creative writer and brainstorm technical solutions for problem X." (Might yield imaginative but technically weak ideas due to role mismatch).
  - *Revised Prompt Snippet:* "Act as an **experienced solutions architect** with a **creative flair**. Brainstorm **technically feasible** solutions for problem X, but don't be afraid to think outside the box." (Role is

now technically grounded but still
encourages creativity).

Revisiting the fundamental structure and the assigned role
are powerful levers when simpler precision tweaks aren't
sufficient.

Reformulating the initial prompt is like going back to the
recipe card and making fundamental changes. But
sometimes, the initial response is mostly good, just needing
targeted adjustments. That's where the power of dialogue
comes in.

Technique 2: Engaging in Dialogue (Follow-up Prompts)

Think of your interaction with the AI less like sending a
command and receiving a final output, and more like
**having a conversation with a very knowledgeable,
literal-minded, but often tireless assistant**. The AI
typically remembers the context of the current conversation
session (up to a certain limit, which varies by model). This
allows you to use short, targeted **follow-up prompts** to
refine, correct, or build upon the AI's *immediately
preceding* response without having to repeat the entire
original prompt. This is the core of the iterative dialogue.

Common Types of Follow-up Prompts:

- **Elaboration/Deepening:**
    - "Can you elaborate on point number 3?"
    - "Tell me more about the you mentioned."
    - "Could you provide more detail on the historical context?"

- **Simplification/Conciseness:**
    - "Can you rephrase that more simply?"
    - "Summarize the key takeaway from your previous response in one sentence."
    - "Make this more concise."

- **Examples/Illustration:**
    - "Give me a concrete example of what you mean by."
    - "Can you illustrate that point with a brief anecdote?"

- **Alternative Perspectives/Counter-arguments:**
    - "What are some potential counter-arguments to this position?"
    - "Could you analyze this from the perspective of?"
    - "Are there alternative solutions you didn't mention?"

- **Correction:**
  - "There seems to be a factual error in the second paragraph regarding. Can you correct it?"
  - "You used informal language, but I requested a formal tone. Please rewrite it formally."
  - "You didn't follow the formatting instruction for the table. Please present it as a table with the specified columns."
- **Style/Tone Adjustment:**
  - "Make the tone more empathetic."
  - "Can you write that in a more persuasive style?"
- **Combination/Synthesis:**
  - "Combine the key ideas from your last two responses into a single paragraph."
  - "Based on our discussion so far, draft a concluding statement."

The beauty of follow-up prompts is their efficiency. You don't need to reconstruct the entire C.R.O.F.T.C structure. You simply provide a targeted instruction referencing the AI's last output. This allows for rapid, incremental refinement.

Co-Constructing the Ideal Response:

This ability to engage in dialogue fundamentally changes the dynamic. You shift from being a passive recipient of AI output to an **active collaborator and guide**. You are no longer just "prompting and praying"; you are actively steering the AI, turn by turn, towards the desired destination.

Imagine sculpting clay. Your initial prompt creates the basic form. The AI's response is the first shaping of the clay. Your follow-up prompts are like your fingers making specific adjustments – smoothing an edge here, adding a detail there, correcting a proportion. Through this back-and-forth, you collaboratively shape the raw potential of the AI's generative ability into a final product that precisely meets your needs, sometimes even exceeding your initial conception as new ideas emerge during the dialogue.

Illustrative Dialogue Scenario:

1. **User (Initial Prompt - C.R.O.F.T.C. based):** "Act as a travel blogger. Write a short (approx. 150 words), engaging paragraph about the appeal of visiting Kyoto, Japan, focusing on the blend of ancient traditions and modern life. Use a slightly evocative tone."

2. **AI (Response 1):** (Generates a decent paragraph mentioning temples, gardens, and modern districts).

3. **User (Follow-up - Refinement):** "That's a good start, but can you make it more specific? Mention Gion district and the feeling of potentially seeing a Geiko. Also, add a sentence about the food scene."

4. **AI (Response 2):** (Rewrites the paragraph, incorporating Gion, the Geiko possibility, and a mention of culinary delights).

5. **User (Follow-up - Tone Adjustment):** "Better! Now, could you make the closing sentence a bit more poetic or reflective?"

6. **AI (Response 3):** (Adjusts the final sentence to be more evocative, e.g., "Kyoto whispers tales of centuries past, even as its modern heart beats vibrantly on.")

Through just two rounds of targeted follow-up, the user guided the AI from a decent but generic response to a much richer, more specific, and stylistically refined paragraph that perfectly matched their evolved vision. This co-constructive dialogue is often the most efficient way to achieve nuanced or complex results.

Mastering both reformulation of the initial prompt and engaging in skillful dialogue provides you with a complete toolkit for iteration. But effectively wielding these tools, especially when faced with initial disappointment, requires a specific mindset.

The Artisan's Mindset: Embracing Growth Through Iteration

How do you react internally when an AI response isn't what you expected? Is your first thought frustration, annoyance, or a judgment about the AI's (or your own) inadequacy? Or do you see it as data, as feedback, as an opportunity to learn and refine?

Successfully navigating the iterative process of prompt engineering benefits enormously from adopting what Stanford psychologist Carol Dweck calls a **"Growth Mindset"**.

Fixed Mindset vs. Growth Mindset:

- A **Fixed Mindset** assumes abilities are innate and fixed. Challenges are threats, effort is fruitless, feedback is criticism, and failure is proof of limitation.

- A **Growth Mindset**, conversely, believes abilities can be developed through dedication and hard work. Challenges are opportunities to grow, effort is the path to mastery, feedback is valuable information, and failure is a lesson learned on the way to success.

Applying Growth Mindset to Prompting:

When you approach prompting with a Growth Mindset:

- **A "failed" prompt isn't a judgment:** It doesn't mean "I'm bad at this" or "The AI is stupid."
- **Failure is information:** It's valuable data about how the AI interpreted your specific instructions in that specific context. It highlights ambiguities you missed, constraints you forgot, or assumptions you made.
- **Every iteration is learning:** Each attempt to reformulate or provide follow-up feedback is an opportunity to better understand how to communicate effectively with this unique intelligence.
- **Effort leads to improvement:** You understand that mastery isn't instantaneous; it comes from practice, experimentation, and learning from mistakes.

This connects strongly to the concept of **metacognition** – thinking about your own thinking. A prompter with a Growth Mindset doesn't just evaluate the AI's response; they reflect on their *own prompting process. "Why did the AI misunderstand that instruction? Was my language unclear? Did I provide enough context? How could I phrase it better next time?"*

Shifting Your Internal Dialogue:

Consciously shift from a fixed-mindset internal monologue to a growth-mindset one:

- **Instead of:** "This is useless! ChatGPT just doesn't get it."
- **Try:** "Okay, this response missed the mark. What specifically was wrong? How did my prompt potentially lead to that? Let me try adding or asking."
- **Instead of:** "I spent so much time on that prompt, and it still failed. I'm just not good at this."
- **Try:** "Interesting. Even with careful planning, the AI interpreted X differently. This shows I need to be even more explicit about. Let's refine and try again – this is part of the learning process."

Adopting this mindset transforms potential frustration into a constructive cycle of learning and improvement. It makes the iterative process less daunting and more engaging. It recognizes that prompt engineering, like any craft, involves continuous learning and refinement. It is the artisan's approach: embracing the process, learning from materials, and persistently working towards excellence.

You are now equipped with the understanding and techniques to handle the inevitable reality that the first prompt isn't always the last. You know that iteration is not failure, but method. You have the tools to analyze AI responses critically, reformulate your initial prompts effectively, engage in productive dialogue through follow-ups, and crucially, maintain a Growth Mindset that turns challenges into learning opportunities.

You've learned to understand the AI, clarify your intent, structure your request, refine the details, and now, iterate towards perfection. You have nearly completed the core training of the prompt pâtissier.

There's one final stage in achieving true mastery and efficiency: moving beyond crafting unique prompts every time to developing your own reusable "signature recipes" – powerful prompt patterns that streamline your workflow for recurring tasks. It's time to learn how to build and leverage your personal prompt library in Chapter 6.

6 - Your Signature Recipes

Creating and Using Effective Prompt Patterns

Through the preceding chapters, you've embarked on a transformative journey. You've learned to understand the AI's predictive "oven" (Chapter 1), clarify your baking intentions (Chapter 2), structure your requests like a detailed recipe card (Chapter 3), master the precision grammage of language and detail (Chapter 4), and embrace the essential art of tasting and adjusting through iteration (Chapter 5). You now possess the core skills of the strategic prompt pâtissier.

You can now confidently approach unique, complex tasks, crafting bespoke prompts tailored to specific situations. But what about the tasks you perform repeatedly? The weekly reports you need to summarize, the types of emails you draft frequently, the brainstorming sessions you regularly conduct, the kinds of analyses you often need? Crafting a detailed, precise prompt from scratch every single time, even with the methods we've learned, can still consume valuable time and mental energy.

This is where the final level of mastery and efficiency comes in: developing your **"signature recipes"**. Just as a master chef doesn't reinvent their base sauces or fundamental doughs every day, the expert prompter develops a collection of reliable, reusable **prompt patterns** – structured templates designed for common tasks, ready to be quickly adapted and deployed.

This chapter introduces the powerful concept of prompt patterns. You'll learn how to identify your own recurring needs that are ripe for templating, explore examples of classic, proven patterns for common professional tasks, discover a practical method for creating and continuously refining your *own* signature prompt recipes, and finally, discuss effective strategies for organizing your growing library of patterns for maximum efficiency and impact. Moving beyond one-off prompts to a system of reusable patterns is the key to unlocking significant, sustainable gains in productivity and consistency.

Beyond the One-Off: Introducing Prompt Patterns

Think about your workflow. How often do you find yourself asking the AI to perform variations of the same fundamental task?

- Summarizing meeting notes or long articles.
- Drafting different types of emails (follow-ups, outreach, announcements).
- Brainstorming ideas (blog topics, marketing angles, problem solutions).
- Comparing options (products, strategies, candidates).
- Explaining complex concepts in simpler terms.
- Extracting specific information from text.

Each time you tackle one of these recurring tasks, you likely go through a similar process of clarifying intent, structuring the prompt, and specifying details. Wouldn't it be more efficient if you had a proven starting point, a pre-built structure specifically designed for that type of task, requiring only minor customization?

That's precisely the idea behind **Prompt Patterns** (also sometimes called prompt templates or archetypes).

A Prompt Pattern is a pre-designed, reusable prompt structure, optimized for a specific type of task or goal. It typically includes:

- **A clear structure:** Often following principles like C.R.O.F.T.C.
- **Core instructions:** Language tailored to the specific task (e.g., instructions for summarizing vs. brainstorming).
- **Placeholders or variables:** Clearly marked sections where you insert the specific details for the current instance (e.g.,,,,).

Think of them like **master recipes in cooking**. A chef has a master recipe for pâte à choux (choux pastry). They don't reinvent it every time they make éclairs or profiteroles. They start with the proven base recipe and then adapt it with specific fillings, glazes, or shaping techniques. Similarly, a prompt pattern for "Summarization" provides the core structure and instructions, and you simply plug in the specific text and desired length or focus for each use case.

This concept also mirrors **design patterns in software engineering** or **templates in document creation**. They are proven solutions to recurring problems, designed to be adapted rather than reinvented each time.

Why Use Prompt Patterns? The Benefits:

- **Massive Time Savings:** Drastically reduces the time spent crafting prompts for common tasks. You start from a proven 80% solution instead of a blank slate.

- **Increased Consistency:** Ensures you apply best practices and include all necessary components every time, leading to more reliable and predictable AI outputs.

- **Improved Quality:** Patterns are often refined over time based on what works best, establishing a higher baseline quality for your results.

- **Easier Delegation/Sharing:** Standardized patterns can be easily shared with team members or assistants, ensuring consistency across an organization.

- **Reduced Cognitive Load:** Frees up mental energy by automating the structuring of routine prompts, allowing you to focus on the specific content and strategic goals.

Visualizing a Simple Pattern:

Imagine a basic pattern for extracting key information:

[--- CONTEXT ---]

The following text is provided:

[Insert Text Here]

[--- ROLE ---]

Act as an efficient information extraction assistant.

[--- OBJECTIVE ---]

Extract the following specific pieces of information from the text provided above:

-

-

-

[--- FORMAT ---]

Present the extracted information as a simple list or key-value pairs.

[--- TONE / STYLE ---]

Factual and concise.

[--- CONSTRAINTS ---]

Extract only the requested information. If any piece of information is not found, state "Not Found".

This pattern provides a clear structure. To use it, you simply replace the bracketed placeholders ([Insert Text Here],, etc.) with the relevant details for each specific use case.

Adopting a pattern-based approach marks a shift from ad-hoc prompting to a more systematic, efficient, and scalable way of interacting with AI. But before you can build your library of patterns, you first need to identify which recurring tasks in *your* workflow would benefit most from having a dedicated template.

What Do You Bake Most Often? Identifying Your Recurring Needs

Prompt patterns are most valuable when applied to tasks you perform repeatedly. Creating a template for a task you only do once a year might not be the best use of your time. The first step, therefore, is to become aware of your own AI usage habits and pinpoint your most frequent or high-value recurring tasks.

How can you identify these prime candidates for pattern creation? Here's a simple self-analysis process:

Step 1: List Your Recent AI Interactions

- Take a few minutes to jot down the last 10-15 distinct tasks you asked an AI (like ChatGPT) to help you with over the past week or two. Be specific. Examples:
    - "Summarized meeting notes from Project X kickoff."
    - "Drafted follow-up email to potential client Y."
    - "Brainstormed blog post titles about topic Z."
    - "Explained complex concept A simply for presentation."
    - "Generated Python code snippet for function B."
    - "Compared features of software C and D."
    - "Rewrote paragraph E to sound more formal."

- "Extracted contact information from article F."
- "Generated ideas for team-building activity G."
- "Analyzed customer feedback H."

Step 2: Group Similar Tasks

- Look at your list and group tasks that fall into the same fundamental category, even if the specific content differed. For instance:
    - **Summarization:** (Meeting notes, articles, reports)
    - **Email Drafting:** (Follow-ups, outreach, announcements, internal comms)
    - **Brainstorming/Idea Generation:** (Titles, topics, solutions, marketing angles)
    - **Explanation/Simplification:** (Complex concepts, technical terms)
    - **Comparison:** (Products, strategies, options)
    - **Rewriting/Tone Adjustment:** (Formalizing, simplifying, making persuasive)
    - **Information Extraction:** (Names, dates, key data points)

○ **Content Creation (Specific Formats):** (Blog posts, social media updates, ad copy, scripts)

Step 3: Identify Your Top 3-5 Categories

- Which categories appear most frequently on your list? Which ones represent tasks that are particularly time-consuming or where consistent quality is crucial? Identify your top 3 to 5 recurring use cases.

- **These are your primary candidates for developing dedicated prompt patterns.** Focusing on these high-frequency tasks will yield the biggest immediate return on your pattern-creation effort.

Connecting to Professional Needs:

Professionals' needs often fall into clear categories that lend themselves well to patterns:

- **Time Optimization:** Summarizing analyses (Consultant), drafting standard clauses (Notary), synthesizing information (RH Manager) – these all scream "Summarization Pattern" or "Drafting Pattern."

- **Content Creation:** Generating fiches produit, ads, emails (E-commerce Entrepreneur), creating course modules or social posts (Coach), drafting podcast summaries (Editor) – these clearly map to "Content Generation Patterns" tailored to specific formats.

- **Strategic Analysis:** Performing due diligence comparisons (Investor), generating financial scenarios (CFO), analyzing legal documents (Lawyer) – these point towards "Comparison Patterns," "Scenario Generation Patterns," or "Information Extraction Patterns."

Your Turn: Find Your Patterns

Pause and perform this self-analysis now.

1. List your recent AI tasks.
2. Group them into categories.
3. Identify your top 3-5 most frequent or important recurring task categories.

Write these down. Knowing *your* specific, high-leverage recurring needs is the essential first step toward building a *personal* library of prompt patterns that will genuinely streamline *your* workflow.

Once you've identified promising candidates, let's explore some classic, battle-tested prompt patterns that you can adapt or use as inspiration.

Classic Patterns from the Prompt Pâtisserie Cookbook

While you'll eventually create highly personalized patterns, it's helpful to start with some common, effective structures that address frequent professional needs. Here are a few examples of classic prompt patterns, presented with their core logic and potential applications:

Pattern 1: The Detailed Persona Pattern

- **Goal:** To ensure the AI deeply embodies a specific role, perspective, or expertise, going far beyond a simple "Act as..." instruction. This is crucial when you need nuanced, expert-level output or a very specific communication style.
- **Structure Breakdown:** Expands significantly on the "Role" component of C.R.O.F.T.C.
- **Template:**

Code extract

```
[ --- CONTEXT --- ]
```

[Provide overall context for the task]

[--- DETAILED PERSONA ---]

You will adopt the following persona for this task:

- **Core Role:**

- **Specialization/Expertise:**

- **Experience Level:**

- **Key Objectives/Priorities:**

- **Target Audience (for your response):**

- **Tone:**

- **Style:**

- **Specific Knowledge/Frameworks to Use (Optional):**

- **Things to Avoid (Optional):**

[--- OBJECTIVE ---]

Based on the persona above, perform the following task:

[State the core task clearly]

[--- FORMAT ---]

[Specify output format]

[--- CONSTRAINTS ---]

[Add any other specific constraints]

- **Example Application (Financial Analysis for CFO):**
  - *Persona Section:* "Core Role: Chief Financial Officer (CFO). Specialization: Tech Startups (SaaS). Experience Level: 10+ years post-IPO experience. Key Objectives: Maximize shareholder value, ensure cash flow runway, mitigate financial risk. Target Audience: Board of Directors. Tone: Cautious, analytical, data-backed. Style: Formal, using standard financial terminology. Things to Avoid: Overly optimistic projections without clear justification."

- *Objective:* "Analyze the attached financial model for Project Phoenix and identify the top 3 financial risks and potential mitigation strategies."
- **Benefit:** This pattern forces the AI to generate responses that are deeply consistent with a specific professional profile, significantly enhancing realism and relevance for expert-level tasks.

Pattern 2: The Structured Comparison Pattern

- **Goal:** To obtain a clear, balanced, and objective comparison between two or more items (products, strategies, candidates, theories, etc.) based on specific criteria. Prevents superficial or biased comparisons.
- **Structure Breakdown:** Focuses on clearly defining items, criteria, and output structure within the Objective and Format sections.
- **Template:**

Code extract

```
[ --- CONTEXT --- ]

[Provide background on why the comparison is needed]

Items to be compared:
```

- Item A:

- Item B:

- (Add more items if needed)

[--- ROLE ---]

Act as a neutral and objective analyst.

[--- OBJECTIVE ---]

Compare Item A and Item B based *only* on the following criteria:

- Criterion 1:

- Criterion 2:

- Criterion 3:

- (Add more criteria as needed)

For each item and each criterion, provide a brief assessment.

[--- FORMAT ---]

Present the comparison in a table format. The columns should be: 'Criterion', 'Item A Assessment', 'Item B Assessment'.

(Alternatively: "Structure the comparison with a separate section for each criterion, discussing Item A and Item B within each section.")

[--- TONE / STYLE ---]

Objective, factual, concise.

[--- CONSTRAINTS ---]

- Base assessments only on provided information or generally known facts (specify if external knowledge is allowed/disallowed).

- (Optional) Conclude with a brief summary highlighting the main differences or a recommendation based *explicitly* on the criteria evaluated.

- **Example Application (Investor Comparing Startups):**
  - *Context:* "Evaluating two B2B SaaS startups for potential seed investment. Startup A:. Startup B:."
  - *Objective:* "Compare Startup A and Startup B based *only* on: 1) Target Addressable Market (TAM) Size estimate, 2) Strength of Founding Team (briefly assess relevant experience), 3) Current Monthly Recurring Revenue (MRR) Traction, 4) Defensibility of Technology."
  - *Format:* "Present comparison in a table with columns: 'Criterion', 'Startup A', 'Startup B'."
  - *Constraints:* "Conclude with an overall risk rating (1-5, 5=highest risk) for each startup based *solely* on these criteria."
- **Benefit:** Ensures comparisons are apples-to-apples, based on defined factors, and presented clearly, facilitating informed decision-making.

Pattern 3: The Guided Brainstorming Pattern

- **Goal:** To leverage the AI as a structured and productive brainstorming partner, moving beyond generic idea lists to generate targeted, creative, and well-defined concepts.

- **Structure Breakdown:** Emphasizes clearly defining the brainstorming goal, desired idea types, quantity, and optional creative constraints.
- **Template:**

Code extract

[--- CONTEXT ---]

[Describe the problem, challenge, or topic for brainstorming]

We are looking for ideas related to.

[--- ROLE ---]

Act as a highly creative and lateral-thinking brainstorming facilitator.

[--- OBJECTIVE ---]

Brainstorm distinct ideas related to the goal stated above.

Focus on ideas that are.

(Optional: Include a mix, e.g., "Generate 5 conventional ideas and 5 highly disruptive ideas.")

[--- FORMAT ---]

Present each idea clearly, perhaps as a numbered list.

For each idea, provide:

- A catchy title or name for the idea.

- A brief (1-2 sentence) description of the core concept.

- (Optional) A note on its potential impact or main benefit.

[--- TONE / STYLE ---]

Creative, open-minded, slightly provocative (if seeking disruptive ideas).

[--- CONSTRAINTS ---]

- (Optional Creative Constraints) e.g., "Assume budget is unlimited," "Consider analogies from the sector," "Focus only on solutions involving community building," "Avoid ideas reliant on third-party integrations."

- (Optional Interaction) "Feel free to ask me 1-2 clarifying questions about the context or constraints if needed before generating the ideas."

- **Example Application (Podcast Editor Seeking Titles):**
  - ○ *Context:* "Brainstorming titles for an upcoming podcast episode about the challenges of remote team communication."
  - ○ *Objective:* "Brainstorm 10 catchy and intriguing titles for this podcast episode. Generate 5 titles that are clear and benefit-driven, and 5 titles that are more provocative or question-based."
  - ○ *Format:* "List the 10 titles. For each, briefly explain the angle or hook."
  - ○ *Constraints:* "Titles should be a maximum of 10 words. Must include the keyword 'remote' or 'virtual'."
- **Benefit:** Transforms the AI from a simple list generator into a genuine creative partner, guided by specific goals and constraints to produce more targeted and imaginative output.

These are just a few examples. Many other patterns exist or can be created for tasks like writing summaries (specifying length, focus, audience), drafting code (defining inputs, outputs, libraries), analyzing text (sentiment, themes, entities), planning projects, and much more.

The key takeaway is that leveraging proven structures for common tasks saves time and improves quality. But the ultimate power comes from moving beyond using *other people's* patterns to creating and refining *your own* signature recipes, perfectly tailored to your unique workflow and needs.

Your Kitchen, Your Recipes: Creating & Refining Your Own Prompt Patterns

While classic patterns provide excellent starting points, the real magic happens when you start transforming your own successful, bespoke prompts into reusable templates – your personal "signature recipes." This allows you to codify what works best *for you* and *your specific recurring tasks*, maximizing efficiency and personalization.

How do you turn a successful one-off prompt into a generic, reusable pattern? Here's a step-by-step method:

Step 1: Identify a "Winner" Prompt

- Look back at your recent AI interactions. Find an instance where you crafted a specific C.R.O.F.T.C. prompt that yielded an exceptionally good result for a task you know you'll need to perform again. This is your candidate prompt.

Step 2: Analyze Its Core Structure and Key Success Factors

- Review the winning prompt. Which parts of the C.R.O.F.T.C. structure were particularly important?
    - Was the detailed Context crucial?
    - Did the specific Role significantly shape the output?
    - Was the clarity of the Objective the key?
    - Did precise Format, Tone, or Constraint instructions make the difference?
- Understand *why* this specific prompt worked so well for that task.

Step 3: Generalize by Replacing Specifics with Variables

- Go through the prompt and identify all the elements that are specific to that *one instance* of the task.

- Replace these specific details with clear, descriptive placeholders or variables, typically enclosed in brackets or similar delimiters.

  - Example: If the prompt said "...analyze sales data for **Q2 2024** for the **European region**...", you might generalize it to "...analyze sales data for for the..."

  - Example: If it specified "...targeting **mid-career professionals**...", generalize to "...targeting..."

  - Example: If the objective was "...draft an email announcing **Product Launch X**...", generalize to "...draft an email announcing..."

- The goal is to remove everything specific to the original case, leaving only the core structure and instructions applicable to *any* instance of that task type.

Step 4: Add Instructions for Using the Template (Optional but Recommended)

- Briefly add comments or notes within or alongside the template explaining what kind of information should go into each variable placeholder. This helps you (or others, if sharing) use the template correctly later.
  - Example: *(Comment: Be specific, e.g., "early-stage tech founders," "HR managers in Fortune 500 companies")*

Step 5: Test and Validate the Template

- Take your newly created pattern and test it on a *different* specific instance of the same task type. Fill in the variables with new details.
- Run the prompt. Does the AI generate a similarly high-quality result? Does the structure hold up?
- This validation step ensures your generalization was successful and the pattern is robust and truly reusable.

Exercise: Create Your First Pattern

1. Choose one of your top recurring tasks identified for Step 1.

2. Find or reconstruct the best prompt you've used for that task so far (even if it wasn't perfect, use the best one).

3. Follow Steps 2-4 above: Analyze it, generalize the specifics into variables, and add brief comments if helpful.

4. (Crucially) Test your new pattern with a different set of specific details for the variables. Does it work? Refine if necessary.

Congratulations! You've just created your first signature prompt recipe. Building these personalized patterns requires a bit of upfront analytical effort, but the payoff in long-term efficiency and consistency is immense.

The Never-Ending Refinement: Keeping Your Recipes Fresh

Just like a chef continually tweaks their signature dishes based on new ingredients, customer feedback, or evolving techniques, your prompt patterns shouldn't be static documents carved in stone. The world of AI is constantly evolving, and so should your patterns.

Embrace Continuous Improvement:

- **Regularly Review:** Periodically revisit your most-used patterns. Are they still producing top-tier results?

- **Note Underperformance:** If a pattern starts yielding less satisfactory outputs, try to diagnose why. Has the underlying AI model been updated, changing how it interprets certain instructions? Is the specific use case slightly different from what the pattern was originally designed for?

- **Adjust and Adapt:** Don't be afraid to tweak your templates based on experience. Maybe a different phrasing for the objective works better now. Perhaps adding a new constraint improves results. Maybe a few-shot example is now needed where it wasn't before.

- **Incorporate New Techniques:** As you learn new prompting strategies (from reading, experimenting, or communities), consider how they could enhance your existing patterns.

- **Version Control (Optional):** For critical patterns, you might even keep track of different versions and what changes were made.

Practical Tip: Your Prompt Recipe Book

Consider keeping a dedicated place to store your personal prompt patterns – your "signature recipe book". This could be:

- A well-organized document on your computer (e.g., Word, Google Doc).
- A section in a note-taking app like Evernote, Notion, or OneNote, using tags for organization.
- A simple text file using clear naming conventions.
- Specialized prompt management tools or browser extensions (explore options if your library becomes large).

Whatever system you choose, make it easy to find, use, and update your patterns. For each pattern, include:

- A clear, descriptive name (e.g., "Pattern - Blog Post Outline Generation," "Pattern - Meeting Summary Extraction").
- The pattern template itself, with clear variables.
- Brief instructions or comments on using it.
- (Optional) Notes on when you last updated it or specific tips for its use.

This iterative refinement ensures your prompt library remains a living, evolving asset that consistently delivers high value, adapting alongside the AI technology itself.

Organizing Your Kitchen: Managing Your Prompt Library

As you create more signature recipes, your collection of prompt patterns will grow. Just like a disorganized kitchen makes cooking stressful and inefficient, a chaotic collection of prompts scattered across random files defeats the purpose of creating reusable assets. **Effective organization is key to maximizing the value and efficiency of your prompt library**.

The Risks of Disorganization:

- **Wasted Time:** Searching through dozens of files or old chat logs to find that perfect prompt you used last month.
- **Reinventing the Wheel:** Re-creating patterns you already built but can't locate.
- **Inconsistency:** Using slightly different versions of the same core prompt without realizing it.
- **Difficulty Sharing:** Unable to easily share best practices or delegate tasks using standardized prompts.

Simple Strategies for Organization:

You don't need a complex system. Choose something simple that works for you and commit to using it consistently. Options include:

1. **Structured Document/File:**
   - Create a single document (e.g., Google Doc, Word) or a dedicated folder.
   - Organize patterns by task category (Summarization, Brainstorming, Email Drafting, etc.) using headings or subfolders.
   - Use clear naming conventions for each pattern file or section.

2. **Note-Taking App (Notion, Evernote, OneNote, etc.):**
   - Create a dedicated notebook or database for your prompts.
   - Use tags to categorize patterns (e.g., #summary, #email, #marketing, #strategy).
   - Leverage the search functionality within these apps.
   - Many allow for easy template creation and duplication.

3. **Text Expansion Utilities:**
   - Tools like TextExpander, Alfred (Mac), or PhraseExpress (Windows) allow you to

store text snippets (your patterns) and insert them instantly using short abbreviations. Highly efficient for power users.

4. **Specialized Prompt Management Tools/Extensions:**

   ○ A growing number of browser extensions and dedicated apps are emerging specifically for storing, organizing, sharing, and even executing prompts. Explore options if your needs become more complex, but start simple.

Key Organizational Tips:

- **Clear Naming:** Give each pattern a descriptive name that clearly indicates its purpose (e.g., "Pattern_Email_FollowUp_ColdLead", "Pattern_Summary_TechnicalArticle_Simple").

- **Add Descriptions:** Include a brief sentence or two explaining what the pattern does and when to use it.

- **Use Variables Consistently:** Adopt a standard way to denote variables (e.g.,, {{Variable Name}}) across all your patterns.

- **Keep it Updated:** When you refine a pattern, update the master version in your library immediately. Delete or archive outdated versions to avoid confusion.

- **Start Simple:** Don't over-engineer your system initially. Choose a method you'll actually maintain.

A well-organized prompt library transforms your collection of signature recipes from a random pile of notes into a powerful, readily accessible toolkit. It makes leveraging your hard-earned prompting expertise fast, efficient, and scalable, truly cementing the productivity gains promised by strategic AI interaction.

You've now completed the full training arc of the prompt pâtissier. You understand the AI, you clarify your intent, you structure your requests, you refine the details, you iterate effectively, and now, you can build and organize your own library of signature recipes. You've moved far beyond the frustration of haphazard "kitchen cooking" with AI. You possess the mindset, the methods, and the techniques to consistently craft prompts that elicit powerful, precise, and valuable results.

But our journey isn't quite over. Before we conclude, let's take a step back and reflect on the broader significance of this newfound skill. How does mastering the art of the prompt translate into a tangible strategic advantage in your professional life? And what does the future hold for this crucial dialogue between human thought and artificial intelligence? Let's turn to the Conclusion.

Conclusion

The Prompt Pâtissier: Your New
Strategic Advantage

We began this journey together facing a paradox: the incredible promise of generative AI contrasted with the often frustrating reality of mediocre or inconsistent results. You, like countless ambitious professionals, sensed the revolutionary potential but felt hampered, unsure how to reliably harness it for your specific, demanding needs. You might have felt like someone handed the keys to a Formula 1 car but only knew how to drive a golf cart.

Remember that initial self-diagnosis from the Introduction? Where did you rate your satisfaction with AI outputs then? Reflect for a moment on how far you've come.

Our guiding metaphor has been the transformation from the haphazard "kitchen sink cooking" of basic prompting to the methodical "precision pastry" of strategic prompt engineering. Let's briefly retrace the essential stages of that transformation, the core skills you've cultivated:

1. **Understanding the Oven (Chapter 1):** You demystified the AI, learning it operates not through understanding but through sophisticated prediction based on context. You grasped the unshakeable GIGO principle and why certain instructions act as powerful steering mechanisms, while also acknowledging inherent limitations like bias and the causal reasoning gap. You learned to see the AI not as magic, but as a logical system to be directed.

2. **Knowing What to Bake (Chapter 2):** You mastered the crucial, often-skipped step of clarifying your *own* intention *before* prompting. Using tools like SMARTE and 5W+H, you learned to translate vague needs into precise, actionable objectives, recognizing that deep thinking is the first and most vital ingredient.

3. **Writing the Recipe Card (Chapter 3):** You discovered the power of structure, learning to organize your clarified intentions into a logical flow using the C.R.O.F.T.C. template. You understood that a well-structured prompt acts like a clear recipe,

guiding the AI reliably and ensuring all components are addressed.

4. **Mastering Precision Grammage (Chapter 4):** You honed your technique, realizing that *every word counts*. You learned to wield precise language, define tone, style, and perspective, specify format and length with intention, use negative constraints effectively, and even leverage the power of examples through few-shot prompting. This is the finesse that elevates output from good to exceptional.

5. **Tasting and Adjusting (Chapter 5):** You embraced iteration not as failure, but as the fundamental method for achieving excellence. You learned to analyze AI responses critically against your goals, skillfully reformulate prompts, and engage in productive dialogue using follow-up questions to co-construct the ideal result.

6. **Creating Signature Recipes (Chapter 6):** You moved beyond one-off prompts to the efficiency of reusable prompt patterns. You learned how to identify your recurring needs, adapt classic patterns, create your own signature templates, and organize your personal library for maximum productivity.

Through this process, you haven't just learned a few tricks for talking to a machine. You have fundamentally transformed your approach to interacting with AI. You no longer prompt haphazardly, hoping for the best. You operate with the intentionality, understanding, and skill of that master pastry chef – knowing your ingredients (context, instructions), understanding your oven (the AI), following a structured method (C.R.O.F.T.C.), applying precise techniques, and iterating until perfection is achieved.

The immediate result? Greater **precision, speed, and quality** in the outputs you generate. Less frustration, less wasted time editing generic responses, and more time leveraging AI to achieve your actual goals – whether that's automating analysis like the Consultant, creating impactful content like the Coach, or accelerating strategic decision-making like the Director General.

Take a moment now to reconsider that initial self-diagnosis. On that 1-to-5 scale, how would you rate your satisfaction and confidence in interacting with AI *now*? Reflect on the specific goal you set for yourself at the end of the Introduction. How much closer are you to achieving it? The progress, hopefully, is palpable.

But the implications of mastering strategic prompt engineering run far deeper than just getting better answers from ChatGPT.

Beyond Technique: Prompting as a Core Cognitive Skill

Let's revisit the insight that has underpinned our entire journey: **A good prompt is not a magic formula; it is a strategy of thought**.

This means the skills you've cultivated throughout this book – the ability to clarify complex intentions, structure thoughts logically, communicate with extreme precision, analyze outputs critically, and iterate based on feedback – are not merely "AI skills". **They are fundamental cognitive competencies.** They are core components of effective thinking, problem-solving, and communication in *any* demanding professional context.

Consider what you've been practicing:

- **Clarifying Intent (Chapter 2):** This is the essence of strategic planning and effective communication. Defining goals clearly before acting is crucial whether briefing a team, planning a project, or writing a persuasive argument.
- **Structuring Thought (Chapter 3):** Organizing information logically, breaking down complexity, and presenting ideas coherently are vital skills for analysis, reporting, and effective management. The

C.R.O.F.T.C. framework is, in essence, a template for structured communication.

- **Precision in Language (Chapter 4):** Choosing words carefully, defining terms, avoiding ambiguity – these are hallmarks of clear thinking and effective influence, critical in fields from law and science to marketing and leadership.

- **Critical Analysis (Chapter 5):** Evaluating information objectively against predefined criteria, identifying flaws or gaps, and providing constructive feedback are essential skills for quality control, decision-making, and continuous improvement.

- **Iteration & Adaptation (Chapter 5):** Learning from feedback, adjusting course based on results, and embracing a process of refinement are fundamental to innovation, skill development, and navigating complexity in any field. The Growth Mindset isn't just for prompting; it's for life.

In essence, learning to prompt strategically is an intensive workout for the core muscles of effective professional thinking. The process of translating your complex human thoughts into instructions an AI can reliably execute forces you to achieve a level of clarity and structure that benefits *all* your intellectual work. As many writers know, the act of writing itself clarifies thought ("Writing is thinking"); similarly, the act of crafting a precise prompt forces you to refine your own understanding of the problem or task at hand.

Think about how these enhanced cognitive skills can ripple outwards:

- The **Consultant** who learns to precisely define the problem for an AI prompt also becomes better at defining the core problem for their human clients.
- The **Manager** who structures clear C.R.O.F.T.C. prompts learns to structure clearer project briefs and delegate tasks more effectively to their team.
- The **Marketer** who crafts prompts specifying precise tone and audience develops a sharper sense of targeted communication in all their campaigns.
- The **Creator** or **Coach** who clarifies their core message for an AI prompt finds it easier to articulate that message powerfully in their own voice across all platforms.

Mastering the prompt isn't just about mastering a tool; **it's about sharpening the most valuable tool you possess: your own mind**. The "strategy of thought" you develop for AI dialogue becomes a transferable asset, enhancing your clarity, effectiveness, and impact across the board.

The Undeniable Competitive Edge

In a world increasingly permeated by artificial intelligence, the ability to dialogue effectively with these powerful tools is rapidly shifting from a niche technical skill to a **fundamental professional competency**. Those who can skillfully leverage AI to amplify their capabilities will inevitably gain a significant advantage over those who cannot.

Why is strategic prompting becoming such a crucial competitive edge?

- **Amplified Productivity:** As studies show, AI assistance can dramatically increase output in various tasks (writing, coding, analysis) *if used effectively*. Strategic prompting is the key to unlocking these productivity gains consistently, freeing up your time for higher-value strategic work.

- **Enhanced Quality:** By guiding the AI with precision, you can achieve a higher quality of output – more insightful analyses, more polished drafts, more relevant ideas – reducing errors and rework.

- **Accelerated Innovation:** Using AI as a structured brainstorming partner (Chapter 6) or exploring diverse perspectives (Chapter 4) can significantly speed up the innovation cycle, allowing you to generate and test ideas faster.

- **Improved Decision-Making:** Leveraging AI for rapid information synthesis, comparison of options, and scenario analysis (guided by well-crafted prompts) can provide richer inputs for more informed and timely decisions.

- **Capability Expansion:** AI allows professionals to perform tasks previously outside their core skillset (e.g., a marketer generating simple code, a writer performing data analysis). Strategic prompting makes this capability expansion more reliable and effective.

The professionals who master this dialogue – who move beyond basic usage to strategic prompting – become **AI-augmented performers**. They are not replaced by AI; they are amplified by it. They become the go-to people in their teams and organizations, the ones who know how to get the most out of these transformative tools. They embody the emerging standard of **AI Literacy**, demonstrating not just awareness, but practical mastery.

Think about your own career trajectory: How could consistently leveraging AI at a higher level of effectiveness differentiate you? Could it help you take on more challenging projects? Deliver results faster and with higher quality? Free up time to focus on leadership, strategy, or client relationships? Position you as an innovator within your field?

The ability to think clearly and translate that clarity into effective instructions for AI is no longer just a "nice-to-have." **It is rapidly becoming a core component of professional competence and a significant driver of career advancement**. Investing time in mastering strategic prompting is not just about learning a new tool; it's a direct investment in your future relevance and competitiveness.

So, how do you ensure this skill becomes not just something you *know*, but something you consistently *do*? How do you weave the practices of the prompt pâtissier into the fabric of your daily work?

Weaving the Craft into Your Daily Workflow: Anchoring the Habits

Knowledge is only potential power; application is real power. Reading this book gives you the understanding and the techniques, but the true benefits emerge only when strategic prompting becomes an ingrained habit, a natural part of your workflow. How can you ensure these practices stick and become second nature?

Like developing any new skill or habit, consistency and deliberate practice are key. It's about integrating small, manageable actions into your routine until they become automatic. Here are some practical ways to anchor the habits of a strategic prompter:

1. **The Two-Minute Rule for Clarity:** Before firing off *any* non-trivial prompt, pause for just one or two minutes. Ask yourself: "What is the *exact* objective here? What does a successful output look like?" Even this brief moment of conscious clarification can significantly improve your prompt's focus.

2. **Structure Becomes Reflex:** For any prompt that involves multiple components (context, specific instructions, format requirements), mentally (or quickly sketch out) the C.R.O.F.T.C. structure. Even if you don't type the headings, consciously thinking through each component ensures you don't miss crucial elements. Make structure the default, not the exception.

3. **Keep Your Checklist Close:** Have your Response Analysis Checklist (from Chapter 5) easily accessible. When you get an AI response, take 60

seconds to run through it. This reinforces critical evaluation and makes iteration more targeted.

4. **Embrace Micro-Iterations:** Don't feel obligated to accept a slightly flawed response just to save time. If an output is 80% there, invest in one or two quick follow-up prompts to push it to 100%. Often, these quick adjustments take less time than fixing the flaws manually later. Normalize the idea of 2-3 iterations for important tasks.

5. **Schedule Pattern Time:** Dedicate just 15 minutes each week (e.g., Friday afternoon) to review, refine, or create prompt patterns for your recurring tasks. This small, consistent investment builds your efficiency engine over time. Treat your prompt library like any other valuable professional asset that requires maintenance.

6. **Reflect Briefly:** After a particularly successful (or unsuccessful) AI interaction, take 30 seconds to reflect: What worked well? What didn't? What did I learn about prompting for *this type* of task? This reinforces the Growth Mindset and accelerates learning.

Your Personal Action Plan:

Don't try to implement everything at once. Choose **ONE** of these habits that resonates most with you or addresses your biggest current challenge in using AI. Commit to practicing just that one habit consistently for the next week. Once it starts feeling natural, pick another. Small, consistent steps are the most effective way to build lasting skills.

Integrating strategic prompting into your daily workflow isn't about adding significant extra time; it's about slightly redirecting your effort towards the highest-leverage activities – clarification, structure, precision, and iteration. It's about working smarter, not just faster. But mastery, like in any craft, requires more than just habit; it requires ongoing learning and adaptation.

The Artisan's Commitment: Continuous Practice and Insatiable Curiosity

The world of artificial intelligence is evolving at breathtaking speed. New models emerge with enhanced capabilities, new prompting techniques are discovered and shared, and the very ways we interact with AI are constantly shifting. Mastering strategic prompting, therefore, is not a one-time achievement; it's an ongoing journey. Like the master chef who never stops experimenting with new ingredients or refining their techniques, the true prompt artisan remains a perpetual student.

Embrace Deliberate Practice:

- **Keep Experimenting:** Don't just rely on the patterns and techniques that work today. Consciously try new approaches. Test different ways of phrasing instructions. Play with varying levels of detail in your context or constraints. Ask the AI to perform tasks slightly outside your comfort zone.

- **Test New Tools:** As new AI models or platforms become available, explore them. How do they respond differently? Do certain techniques work better or worse with different models? Understanding the nuances of various tools broadens your adaptability.

- **Seek Feedback (Implicitly):** Pay close attention to the AI's responses as feedback not just on the content, but on your prompt itself. If an AI consistently misunderstands a certain type of instruction, take that as feedback to refine your phrasing.

Cultivate Curiosity:

- **Stay Informed:** Follow reputable sources (blogs, newsletters, research papers, expert communities) discussing advancements in AI and prompt engineering. Understanding where the technology is heading helps you anticipate future shifts in best practices.

- **Learn from Others:** Engage with communities of practice (online forums like Reddit, specialized Discord servers, professional groups) where users share successful prompts, innovative techniques, and lessons learned. The collective intelligence of the prompting community is a powerful resource.

- **Ask "What If?":** Maintain a playful, inquisitive spirit. What if I asked the AI to combine two unrelated concepts? What if I gave it contradictory instructions? What if I prompted it using only questions? Curiosity drives discovery.

Set Small Challenges:

- To keep your skills sharp and continuously learn, consider setting yourself small, regular prompting challenges. For example:

- o This week, try using few-shot prompting for a task you usually handle with descriptive instructions.
- o This month, try automating one small, recurring task using a new prompt pattern you develop.
- o Explore a new AI model or feature and see how its prompting differs from what you're used to.

Lasting mastery in any dynamic field comes not just from initial learning, but from this commitment to **deliberate practice and persistent curiosity**. It requires the humility to recognize that there's always more to learn, and the drive to continually refine your craft in response to an ever-evolving landscape. This commitment ensures that your prompting skills remain sharp, relevant, and powerful, today and into the future.

And what might that future look like?

The Dialogue Evolves: Your Role in the Future of Human-AI Collaboration

The rapid advancement of AI inevitably raises questions about the future of prompting. Will AI become so sophisticated that it perfectly understands our vaguest intentions, rendering careful prompting obsolete?

Perhaps partially. Future AI models will likely become better at inferring context, asking clarifying questions proactively, and handling ambiguity. The mechanics of interaction might change – perhaps more voice interaction, more intuitive interfaces, AI agents that take multi-step actions based on high-level goals.

However, the fundamental need for **human clarity of thought and strategic direction is unlikely to disappear**. Why?

- **Complexity Remains:** As AI tackles increasingly complex tasks, the need to accurately define the problem, set nuanced goals, and specify critical constraints will remain paramount. Ambiguity doesn't scale well with complexity.
- **Quality Requires Guidance:** While AI might get better at producing *something* from a vague request, achieving *specific, high-quality, tailored* results that meet demanding professional standards will likely always benefit from precise human guidance. Think bespoke tailoring versus off-the-rack clothing.

- **Strategic Intent is Human:** AI can execute tasks, but the underlying strategic goals, the creative vision, the ethical considerations – these originate from human intention. Effectively translating that intent into actionable guidance for the AI will remain a crucial human skill.

- **The Amplification Factor:** The more powerful the AI becomes, the *more* critical the quality of human guidance and oversight becomes. Steering a super-intelligent system requires greater skill and responsibility than steering a simple one. Small imprecisions in prompts could lead to larger deviations in output.

Therefore, the core skills you've developed throughout this book – clarifying intent, structuring thought, communicating precisely, analyzing critically, iterating effectively – are likely to become **even more valuable** in the future. They represent the enduring human side of the human-AI equation. Even if the interface changes, the need for **clear thinking as the input to intelligent systems** will persist.

Imagine your interaction with AI five years from now: Perhaps you're verbally briefing an AI assistant on a complex project. Even without typing, will you need to clearly articulate the objectives? Define the key constraints? Structure your briefing logically? Specify the desired outcome and audience? Almost certainly, yes. The *medium* might change, but the underlying *mental discipline* of strategic prompting will remain essential.

The future belongs to those who can think clearly and partner intelligently with artificial intelligence. Those who master this dialogue will be best positioned to leverage AI's escalating capabilities, driving innovation, productivity, and impact in ways we are only beginning to imagine.

The Prompt is the Beginning

We've reached the end of our structured journey, but it's truly just the beginning of yours. You began, perhaps, with a sense of frustration or untapped potential in your interactions with AI. Through understanding, structure, precision, and iteration, you've transformed that relationship. You are no longer just a user; you are a strategic director, a collaborator, a prompt pâtissier capable of crafting interactions that yield truly exceptional results.

The core message, the insight, bears repeating one last time: **prompting is a strategy of thought**. The techniques and templates are valuable tools, but the real power lies in the sharpened clarity, structured thinking, and intentionality you bring to the process. This is a skill that extends far beyond your interactions with ChatGPT, enriching your communication, problem-solving, and strategic thinking in all areas of your professional life.

As you continue to practice and refine your craft, remember the responsibility that comes with this power. Use your ability to guide these powerful tools ethically and wisely. Strive for accuracy, fairness, and positive impact in the outputs you generate and the ways you employ them.

The dialogue between human intelligence and artificial intelligence is one of the defining narratives of our time. By mastering the art of the prompt, you are not just learning a technical skill; you are becoming a more effective participant in that conversation, a **co-author** of the future we are creating together with these remarkable tools.

Thank you for embarking on this journey. Now, go forth, practice your craft with intention and curiosity, and continue to refine your own unique signature recipes. The world – and the AI – awaits your clear, strategic, and impactful prompts.

I'd Love to Hear Your Thoughts.

If this book resonated with you—if it challenged you, inspired you, or gave you a new perspective—I'd truly appreciate it if you shared your thoughts in a review.

Not only does your feedback mean a lot to me, but it also helps others who might be looking for this kind of message. Even just a few words can make a difference.

If you feel like it, you can leave a review by scanning the QR code or typing the link below.

Thank you for reading, and for being part of this journey.

https://authorhelp.uk?azr=B0F3WF9141

www.ingramcontent.com/pod-product-compliance
Lightning Source LLC
LaVergne TN
LVHW051323050326
832903LV00031B/3341